Crisis Management

Crisis Management

Effective School Leadership to Avoid Early Burnout

Larry Dake

ROWMAN & LITTLEFIELD
Lanham • Boulder • New York • London

Published by Rowman & Littlefield
An imprint of The Rowman & Littlefield Publishing Group, Inc.
4501 Forbes Boulevard, Suite 200, Lanham, Maryland 20706
www.rowman.com

6 Tinworth Street, London, SE11 5AL, United Kingdom

Copyright © 2021 by Larry Dake

All rights reserved. No part of this book may be reproduced in any form or by any electronic or mechanical means, including information storage and retrieval systems, without written permission from the publisher, except by a reviewer who may quote passages in a review.

British Library Cataloguing in Publication Information Available

Library of Congress Cataloging-in-Publication Data

Names: Dake, Larry, 1980– author.
Title: Crisis management : effective school leadership to avoid early burnout / Larry Dake.
Description: Lanham, Maryland: Rowman & Littlefield, 2021. | Includes bibliographical references. | Summary: "This book will assist school leaders with strategies to navigate transitions, balance relationships, and manage their time more effectively"— Provided by publisher.
Identifiers: LCCN 2020045777 (print) | LCCN 2020045778 (ebook) | ISBN 9781475859553 (cloth) | ISBN 9781475859584 (paperback) | ISBN 9781475859591 (ebook)
Subjects: LCSH: School administrators—Job stress—United States. | School management and organization—United States. | Educational leadership—United States.
Classification: LCC LB2831.62 .D35 2021 (print) | LCC LB2831.62 (ebook) | DDC 371.2/0110973—dc23
LC record available at https://lccn.loc.gov/2020045777
LC ebook record available at https://lccn.loc.gov/2020045778

Contents

Preface		vii
Introduction: Preparing School Leaders Effectively		ix
1	The Grass May Look Different, But It's Not Always Greener . . . One Administrator's Story	1
2	Was It Always This Way? School Leadership's Unique History	5
3	You Are Contagious . . . for Better or Worse	11
4	Without This, Schools Cannot Move Forward: Building Trusting Relationships	17
5	Making It All Fit: Professional Fit and Work-Life Balance	27
6	Is It Lonely at the Top? Navigating Leadership Isolation and Loneliness	37
7	Preparing for the Shift and Navigating New Roles	47
8	Survey Overview, Important Trends, and Takeaways	57
9	The Goose That Lays the Golden Egg: School Leadership and Time Management	63
10	Is It Time to Seek a New Opportunity? Interviewing and Entry Planning	73

**11 Must-Read Books for Prospective and Practicing
School Leaders**   83

Appendix: Survey Instrument   93

About the Author   97

Preface

School leaders possess the necessary agency to navigate their job's inherent stress. Stress cannot be eliminated wholly and is part of the deal to accept when moving from individual contributor to manager; assistant principals, principals, and district office leaders are responsible for hundreds, if not thousands, of people's well-being on a daily basis. This responsibility should neither be taken lightly nor dismissed as unrelated to the job. When educators pursue their administrative certificates and accept administrative positions, they also accept the fact that their responsibility levels will increase dramatically and their professional and personal lives will change. As responsibility increases, so too will occupational stress.

Specific approaches and strategies exist for school leaders to help navigate their occupational stress. They can create conditions to pursue better work-life balance, self-care, and by extension, their school community's well-being. As aforementioned, a healthy school leader has a dramatic impact on a healthy school community. Creating these conditions is within the reach of each school leader, regardless of position, title, level of authority, or years of experience.

Beginning and veteran administrators may benefit from practicing these approaches and strategies. By identifying research-based methods as well as those implemented by practitioners in the field, this work is applicable to all school leaders. In particular, prospective and beginning administrators should attend these approaches and strategies as they undergo the challenging transition that accompanies one when they move from individual contributor to a larger system (i.e., classroom teacher) to being responsible for large parts of the system itself.

The motivation for this book was drawn from personal experience. My first transition occurred at age thirty when I was promoted within the same organization from teacher to district-level administrator. August 21, 2010, was my first day and, on that day, seven people who attended my wedding three years earlier "unfriended" me on Facebook. It seems silly now, but at the time it hurt. The only change was that I "went to the dark side." In retrospect, I know I should have expected this, but at the time it was jarring.

Beyond my school leadership duties, I also teach educational leadership courses at the graduate level. While our offerings are relevant for prospective administrators, we still do not prepare students for these transitions. Friendships change. Relationships are altered. Those who you thought had your back no longer do. Leadership has far more rewards than regrets, but these dynamics should be discussed in our courses.

This book relies on two data sources to tease out these dynamics. First, several new and veteran school leaders were interviewed. Throughout these interviews, common themes emerged and will be highlighted. Second, a survey was conducted for beginning and veteran school leaders that asked them to dive deeply into several questions around stress, responses, and strategies. Both of these data sources complement each other and provide different windows into the same topic.

Introduction
Preparing School Leaders Effectively

Educational Law. Curriculum Development. Leadership Theory. Evaluation and Supervision. Upon entry into a school leadership preparation program, most students work through courses designed to instruct them in topics such as these. These topics are, of course, vital to an understanding of administration, management, and school leadership. They touch upon several vital elements that are encompassed within the broad field upon which successful candidates will embark when they are hired for their first administrative position. Success in this field, however, often rests not upon these topics, but upon the grey areas that mark a school leader's day-to-day experience.

Stress management and avoiding burnout. Dealing with difficult staff members. Keeping a cool head when the pressure is on. Knowing when to transition to a new opportunity. Recognizing that you don't have all of the answers, and nor should you. These are areas that make or break school leaders. When school leaders fail to navigate a difficult culture and when their schools do not experience successful outcomes, more often than not it may relate to one of these areas.

Unlike the first category, there may not be "go-to" people within the organization for guidance. While principals can contact their district offices for advice on a personnel problem the italicized items often come from within personal and professional makeup. While they can be taught and learned, they also result from the sum of an administrator's personal and professional experience, background, and philosophy.

School leadership can be isolating and lonely. Often, a building principal is the only administrator within a building. A collective bargaining unit's unifying forces usually do not apply. Regardless of position within an organization, they may be the *only* professional in their particular role, or be among a very small number who occupy that position across a school district.

School leaders need to be intentional about taking care of themselves. Teachers and related staff often embark upon a career in school leadership because they want to make a difference in the lives of students and staff. The boundaries between continual giving and intentional self-care are easily blurred. When school leaders take a vacation, for example, the school community home can find you, e-mail you, and may even call you. When Saturday morning rolls around, the problems left behind on Friday afternoon are not far off. The organization for which you work may provide you with a district-issued smartphone—truly a blessing and a curse.

"Securing your own mask first," as a concept, came about in conversation with several school leaders. Some of these leaders are wonderful at their jobs and, simultaneously, incredibly close to burnout. Others have found themselves in ideal fits for their stage of life and understand that balance is the ultimate goal. Still others find themselves somewhere in between those two extremes. As this book unfolded in planning and practice, and the accompany survey data was analyzed, several themes emerged that will be useful for school leaders who want to be more intentional about their own work-life balance and self-care.

Moreover, those considering leadership as a career path will also benefit from the pages that follow. The required classes are necessary, but they are not the entire story that should be considered when thinking about a move from individual contributor within a system to taking on responsibility for that system.

This book will unfold by outlining several themes relevant to those considering an administrative career and those already within a formal school leadership position. It will begin with Greg's story—a veteran administrator who has made several transitions within his career. Some of these have been successful, and some have not. Greg's story is illustrative of the push and pull many school leaders feel when considering whether to remain in a good fit or take a more prestigious position. It also highlights several areas prospective school leadership should consider when starting their classes or applying for that first formal position.

Then, school leadership itself will be examined historically. Over the years, the role of the "principal teacher" in the 1920s has evolved into a job that many researchers consider "too big for one." While this chapter will center specifically on the principalship, its lessons apply to other formal titles as well. In light of this evolution, research on occupational stress, burnout, and related topics will be considered within the chapter. It is important to consider "why" school leaders often face high levels of loneliness, burnout, and other challenges.

After considering this research, the next several chapters are organized around themes that emerged from interviews and survey responses. These chapters will highlight the research undertaken to uncover how school leaders feel about their jobs, what burns them out, and what is so rewarding about the job that administrators can walk back into the office every day. In addition, this research points to several important ideas that school leaders can implement to practice intentional self-care, avoid burnout, and be more effective as a school leader, a husband/wife, a parent, and a member of the greater community.

Finally, we will highlight "toolbox" items such as time management practices, entry planning, and key additional readings. If any one word encapsulates the strategies that school leaders can employ to avoid burnout, it is "relationships." This will be revisited continually throughout this book.

Overall, dozens of school leaders contributed to this work. Whether through in-person interviews, phone calls, or the survey data, these ideas could not have been brought to fore without broad-based feedback. School leaders need to take care of themselves.

Chapter 1

The Grass May Look Different, But It's Not Always Greener...

One Administrator's Story

Whenever he had the opportunity, Greg beelined to his principal's office to participate on building-level teams, ask questions about scheduling, or observe his veteran leader's ability to have difficult conversations. Greg was a twenty-two-year-old, fresh elementary teacher who was already planning his entry into school leadership. Lucky for Greg, he had access to an experienced principal more than willing to help him broaden his perspective. Over the next five years, Greg spent countless hours in this leadership incubator as he pursued his own administrative degree.

Greg's leadership story truly has it all. It contains tales of strong mentors, supportive and unsupportive district offices, successful transitions, and those gone awry. Over his sixteen years in school leadership, Greg has worked as an administrator in three districts and transitioned from central office to the principalship and back again. Greg's story contains valuable lessons for aspiring and practicing school leaders. Among them, "the grass is not always greener on the other side of the fence" and "fit" are perhaps the most important attributes for school leaders to consider when thinking through a transition to a new position.

After five years as teacher and approaching age thirty, Greg was hired in as a district-level leader in a different organization. Greg's title encompassed "special programs," and it quickly became apparent that every new initiative had something "special" to it. Greg's plate became larger and larger at the same that he and his wife started their family.

Despite this, Greg thrived in this environment. A new superintendent and an experienced assistant superintendent provided strong mentoring and support. Ultimately, however, Greg yearned for a leadership opportunity at a building level. After five years directing special programs, Greg applied for and was hired as a building principal in yet another organization.

Greg inherited a building with significant leadership turnover in recent years. He was immediately welcomed as a stabilizing force. Greg's energy and empathy quickly resonated with students and staff. His impact was immediate. His school community embraced his visible, hands-on approach.

Moreover, the school was small enough for an energetic principal to quickly learn everyone's story. Similar to his previous district, Greg enjoyed strong superintendent and assistant superintendent support. In fact, in reflecting on his journey, Greg stated, "One area that has struck me in all of my transitions is how district office can make or break you. It's not so much whether they like you or not, but are they going to stand up for you. I've learned from both having that support, and then not having it."

Four years after turning his building around, Greg's district experienced turnover at both the superintendent and assistant superintendent positions. With the district in flux, a new opportunity for Greg arose. A district-level position in a neighboring district opened and Greg was hired. Leaving a building that had already experienced high turnover was difficult, but Greg faced this transition has he had his previous ones: eager to learn and ready to work. This transition, however, would be unlike others.

In his new position, his phone never stopped pinging after 5:30 p.m. It always seemed like some stakeholder needed something from Greg. Although he was brought into bring change to the system, the district demonstrated that it was mired in a comfortable status quo. With a predominantly school-ready population, test scores were above average. Staff was comfortable. Change was not an endeavor many staff members felt was necessary. Greg soon ran headlong into opposition not only from rank-and-file staff, but from his administrative colleagues, as well. Greg reflected, "I sort of became the target because the superintendent couldn't be the target. He's the superintendent. So as the new guy, it really became me."

In particular, building principals refused to implement the changes that Greg was pursuing, despite that they were being approved behind the scenes by the superintendent. It all came to a head in a three-way meeting between a recalcitrant principal, Greg, and Greg's superintendent. Greg remembers that "the principal went up one side of me and down the other. And the superintendent, while I like him personally quite a bit, did not intervene. That's when I knew it was over." Greg had experienced strong superintendent support in two previous positions. In this case, however, he did not.

Greg put a call into his former superintendent. Would they possibly consider taking him back? Within weeks, Greg was back in his old building as principal. "It really came down to fit and where I wanted to be at this stage in my life," Greg reflected. "I didn't have a life anymore and it was starting to impact my personal life." Upon returning, those staff bonds that were built grew stronger. According to Greg, "I know I don't have to walk into this building with a target on my back. We support each other."

Greg's story is an ideal starting place because it encompasses many themes to be explored. The following are a few of them.

NAVIGATING TRANSITIONS

During Greg's twenty-one-year educational career, he has experienced several transitions. He has gone from elementary teacher to district office. Then, he moved from a district office position to a principalship, and then from another district-level position back to his original building as principal. Greg's story underlines how important district office support can be when navigating a transition and attempting to implement change. Throughout this book, navigating transitions will be continuous theme. A school leader's ability to navigate power relationships within an organization can make or break success.

Greg's story is buttressed by the survey data we will analyze throughout this text. Nearly 60% of respondents reported being untenured in their current position; therefore, most of those surveyed have less than four years in their current administrative position. Transitions are a part of leadership's journey for those who undertake them. These professional transitions also occur within personal transitions. For example, less than 10% responded that they were single while over 60% reported having young children at home. Accepting more professional responsibility should be viewed within ongoing personal transitions at home.

PROFESSIONAL FIT

It is important to understand that not all positions are created equal. While some positions may have more leadership authority, have a higher salary, or be the right "step" on a path toward a higher position, they may not be the right fit for every person at every time. Greg learned this when he left his principalship. He quickly discovered that district culture and resistance to change can erode one's perceived fit for a position. Throughout the stories discussed in this book, professional fit and its relation to one's work-life balance will be continual themes.

Throughout the survey, several respondents listed professional fit as a challenge. In listing their top stressors, responses such as "lack of district vision," "unrealistic expectations by supervisor," and similar comments were among respondents' top indicators. More importantly, when asked which stressors they perceive possessing little control over, many building-level administrators listed their frustrations with district offices. Scanning open positions for perceived fit can help identify good opportunities.

RELATIONSHIPS

Most importantly, Greg's story underscores the importance of relationships. Building a strong culture with staff is the primary buffer against professional loneliness. In his building Greg is the only administrator among several teachers, aides, and clerical staff. He is the one who must make final decisions about student management, safety, and learning. As Greg reflected, he and his staff are not best friends. However, he has built relationships based on mutual respect and symbiosis.

For example, when Greg hurt his foot and wasn't able to come to work for a week, his staff missed him. They missed his professional presence and how that positively impacted their classrooms. Trusting relationships are centered on around respect and mutual need. School leaders need strong staff, and staff need strong school leaders.

Finally, Greg's long-standing relationship with his staff is a major buffer against loneliness and burnout. Among survey respondents, approximately 50% reported less than three years' experience in their current position. Building sustainable relationships can take time and Greg's story illustrates that the journey toward those relationships can be nonlinear. Jumping to new career opportunities can help administrators climb the ladder, but the trade-off may be a lack of sustainable relationships among staff and community members.

In the next chapter, school leadership will be viewed within its historical context. Over the decades, school leadership, and particularly the principalship, has become a job many consider "too big for one." The current school leadership role has evolved considerably, due to many factors, over the preceding decades. This evolution has contributed to school leaders being highly susceptible to stress and burnout, in particular, without intention steps to mitigate their impacts.

Chapter 2

Was It Always This Way?
School Leadership's Unique History

EXPECT TO LEARN

In this chapter, the reader can expect a historical overview of school leadership over the last hundred years. Over that time, school systems and leadership responsibilities have grown more complex. Both historical circumstances and increased political regulation have contributed to increased complexity.

Since the 1980s, several factors have contributed to increased workload and stress levels. To better understand how school leadership arrived at this present moment, it will be helpful to consider its evolution into a full access and full service occupation for students, staff, and communities. Increased roles and responsibilities coincide with the growth in mass schooling and the increase in students' legal rights within the school system.

When American schooling began, of course, the principalship as we know it today did not exist. Small schoolhouses dotted the American landscape for over a century before urbanization and industrialization brought a new complexity to the national lifestyle. As formal education became less an affluent child's expectation and more a democratic norm, schools outgrew the rural one-room schoolhouses and grew more complex. Only in the 1920s did a formal recognition of the "principal teacher" become realized through early professional organizations.[1]

The pre–World War II era witnessed scientific management's rise and early attempts to measure and dissect American society on a national scale. The literature describes school leaders as "leaders of technical workers" while educational authors connected American schooling to the World War I era achievement testing intended to categorize soldiers into ranks.

During this time, school leadership emerged as a separate career path within the educational field and a separate professional space from classroom teaching. The language used to describe school leadership closely mirrored the language used to describe business leaders. School principals were expected to be rational managers who employed scientific means to lead their schools through benevolent authoritarianism.

American schooling took on more moralistic tones during World War II with dramatic implications for school leaders. As teenagers fought against Nazi Germany in Europe and Imperial Japan in the Far East, the classroom became a breeding ground for democratic themes.[2] Education was popularly viewed as the means to make democracy work for all American citizens. This democratic spirit extended to intraschool power structures as well.

Throughout the 1940s, flattered hierarchies and teacher involvement in decision-making were emphasized. Fighting authoritarianism abroad called for more democratic themes at home. The era's tone, however, masked the underlying discrimination experienced by disadvantaged groups throughout the United States. As World War II ended and America emerged victorious, movements abroad in society would have far-reaching implications for schools.

From the 1920s to the 1940s, school leadership took small steps toward becoming a formalized, separate career path. The 1950s witnessed rapid growth in this area as school administration preparation programs emerged to train a new crop of leaders. As "central offices" emerged to handle budget, curriculum, and management as separate issues, school leaders were expected to act as skilled administrators applying general theories to their work.[3]

A dual role emerged in the 1950s: to apply objective, research-based practices to school administration, and to plan and organize school life and events. The 1990's movement toward accountability has strong antecedents in the 1950's emphasis on scientific study, empirical evidence, and rational management.

As the 1960's social upheaval unfolded, school administration developed as a bulwark to support rational approaches to administration. During the 1960s, a well-developed educational bureaucracy took shape as with clear lines of power and responsibility.[4] For the first time in the literature, classroom instruction supervision emerged as a theme.

Moreover, school integration efforts increased after the 1954 *Brown vs. Board of Education*. In addition, the mid-to-late 1960s witnessed organized public-sector teacher unions; in the Northeast United States, in particular, unionization brought a further fracture between administration and teaching as separate but related career paths. Finally, at the federal level, legislation such as the 1965 Elementary and Secondary Schools Act greatly expanded the federal government's role in school accountability.

The mid-to-late 1960s proved a watershed for school leadership and provided the antecedents for the current all-inclusive administrative job title. The

1970s continued this change apace. During this decade, school integration continued rapidly and new federal mandates such as the 1975 Individuals with Disabilities in Education Act further expanded oversight and accountability. With rapid social change impacting schools, ensuring student and staff self-actualization was a dominant theme.

Moreover, transformational leadership themes were foreshadowed in this era as educational equity emerged as a theme. School administrators were expected to incorporate increasing diverse student bodies into cohesive wholes with several new paradigms such as "classrooms without walls." While academic accountability did not disappear, it took a back seat to humanistic tones.[5]

An accountability backlash was close behind as the 1983 *A Nation at Risk* reported that American schooling was failing internationally. Moreover, the report situated responsibility for leading change squarely on the principal as the "change agent." School leaders emerged as central figures in a "crisis tone" that swept through education.[6] America's position in the world was seemingly threatened and the nation's schools were expected to meet this challenge. Accountability became a major theme as principals were expected to be *the*, not just *a*, major influence on the school.

Principals leading the learning process for their teachers emerged as a major theme as the word "intervene" first appeared in the school lexicon. In many ways, these themes mirrored the "principal teacher" role that school leaders played in the 1920s, but with one major exception: in that era, the "principal teacher" was one of many school leaders as other teachers, too, participated in a flattered hierarchy.

As the Effective Schools movement took hold in the 1980s, however, school leaders and especially principals were now expected to be "the" school leader. Further divisions between teachers and administrators opened in collective bargaining as these two roles further splintered. A clear hierarchy emerged with the school leader directing the school's activities and teachers expected to carry out those directives. The school leader as change agent, community-builder, defender of student rights, motivator, professional developer, data analyzer, and any other "jack-of-all-trades" terms congealed in this era.

These instructional leadership themes continued and were joined by more transformational themes as the Cold War ended in the early 1990s. Shared decision-making models and other distributive leadership models emerged to meet a postindustrial world and its needs. More than an instructional leader utilizing business models, principals were tasked as "head learners" in ways reminiscent of the 1920s.

Of course, schools were much more complex in the 1990s than they were seven decades earlier. Themes such as servant leadership, distributive leadership, and democratic leadership became relevant in the literature alongside that from the 1980s Effective Schools movement.

The 1990s can be viewed as an attempt to merge the 1980's instructional leadership themes with those from earlier eras emphasizing self-actualization. National governors met in the early 1990s to commit to increase accountability measures and several states ushered mandated common assessments. In the late 1990s, for example, grades four and eight mandated standardized testing emerged in many states.

While not yet tied to school accountability sticks and carrots, these early standardized tests represented a significant change in school evaluation. During the 1990s, while schools experienced flattered hierarchies internally, mandated accountability systems were taking shape; these systems would have profound impacts on school leaders' workload and job responsibilities.

In 2001, No Child Left Behind (NCLB) mandated annual grades three through eight testing. Although grades four and eight exams began in the 1990s, NCLB's annually increasing achievement levels and accountability system of rewards and punishments further intensified leadership work. While earlier accountability systems did publicize results, they did so without rankings systems and labels such as "schools in need of improvement." In addition, NCLB set ever-increasing achievement levels for schools to attain over time until 100% of all students were deemed proficient in English Language Arts and Mathematics.

This was a watershed moment that transformed school leadership forever. It is this combination of external assessments *plus* ever-increasing external accountability that heightened school leadership complexity. It was no longer enough to build a positive school culture, practice transformational leadership, develop strong relationships, among other needs. With NCLB, and subsequently Race to the Top during the Obama administration, meeting external accountability measures became crucial to maintaining a positive school-wide and personal leadership reputation.

The school leadership literature reflected this shift. During this time, school leadership became recognized as the "catchall" needed to raise test scores, develop transformational leadership practices, keep students and staff safe, among other dynamics. Representative is Marks and Printy's[7] "shared instructional leadership" model for the role that school leaders, and especially principals, play in their organization's daily life. Marks and Printy criticize the 1980s Effective Schools movement as too leadership-centric and undervaluing the shared efforts of all school staff.

Similarly, they cast aside the 1990s focus on transformational leadership practices as too removed from student achievement. Their shared model views the school leader as the "facilitator" of school success rather than its primary driving force or inspector.[8] They urge school leaders to be transformational leaders who accept their instructional role and exercise it in collaboration with teachers. They "cohere in practice"[9] by working simultaneously as transformational and instructional leaders. These themes dominate the school leadership literature over the last two decades.

Other authors have echoed this call for school leaders to play a "facilitator" role in promoting student success. Robinson and Temperedly[10] identified "promoting and participating in teacher learning and development" as having the highest effect size for leadership practices. They urge school leaders to not view themselves as "hero" leaders but rather focus on behaviors that facilitate their teachers becoming better instructors.

Instructional leadership tasks and working alongside teachers become one and the same. Research has identified three "basic principles of leadership": setting direction, developing people, and redesigning the organization. Researchers have also found that a school leader's sense of collective efficacy had a strong and positive relationship with shared instructional leadership practices.[11]

Moreover, Hellinger and Heck identified a "mutual influence process" among school leaders and their staff whereby capacity is built collectively in a dynamic, not static, model.[12] All and all, the school leadership literature over the last two decades has identified the need for school leaders to develop teacher and staff leadership while simultaneously charging into their instructional role to promote student achievement.

The research cited above focuses on the school leader's role in relation to their instructional tasks and staff development; it does not account for several other dynamics that have intensified their work. Over the last twenty years, school violence has developed into a national conversation with schools now practicing lockdown and active shooter drills.

Moreover, national conversations about student mental health have led to schools being responsible for not only addressing bullying but preventing it from happening in the first place. Rising poverty rates have intensified focus on school breakfast and lunch practices and schools have been tasked with addressing childhood obesity rates.

Furthermore, shrinking budgets have caused schools and districts to promote efficiencies in any way possible. All in all, school leaders enter the next decade responsible for, among other things, increasing each student's achievement level, empowering their staffs to improve their practices, keeping all students and staff safe from external and internal forces, feeding children healthy meals, and reducing costs as much as possible. It is no wonder that more and more school leaders spend time fending off burnout while attempting to fulfill an almost impossible "catchall" position.

This chapter focused on school leadership historically and the forces which have shaped, and continue to shape, the professional and those within it. It is important to understand how school leadership has changed over the last hundred years to fully grasp the role's current pressures and challenges. As we will see in the next chapter, the unique stressors faced by school leaders make them increasingly prone to mental health challenges, burnout, and related challenges. We will discuss occupational stress experienced by school leaders and how these dynamics coincide with research on mental health challenges and burnout.

NOTES

1. L. G. Beck and J. Murphy, *Understanding the Principalship: Metaphorical Themes 1920s-1990s* (New York: Teacher's College Press), 1993, 1–2.
2. Beck and Murphy, *Understanding the Principalship: Metaphorical Themes 1920s-1990s*, 32–34.
3. Beck and Murphy, *Understanding the Principalship: Metaphorical Themes 1920s-1990s*, 91–94.
4. Beck and Murphy, *Understanding the Principalship: Metaphorical Themes 1920s-1990s*, 113–114.
5. Beck and Murphy, *Understanding the Principalship: Metaphorical Themes 1920s-1990s*, 121–128.
6. John Goodland, "The Uncommon Common School," *Education and Urban Society*, 16, no. 3 (1984): 243–252.
7. M. Marks and M. Printy, "Principal Leadership and School Performance: The Integration of Transformational and Instructional Leadership," *Educational Administration Quarterly*, 39 (2003): 370–397.
8. Marks and Printy, "Principal Leadership and School Performance," 381–382.
9. Marks and Printy, "Principal Leadership and School Performance," 391.
10. Vivian M. J. Robinson and Helen Temperedly, "The Leadership of the Improvement Teaching and Learning: Lessons from Initiatives with Positive Outcomes for Students," *Australian Journal of Education*, 51, no. 3 (2007): 247–262.
11. K. Leithwood and D. Janzi, "Linking Leadership to Student Learning: The Contributions of Leader Efficacy," *Educational Administration Quarterly*, 44, no. 4 (2008): 496–528.
12. Phillip Hellinger and Ronald Heck, "Leadership for Learning: Does Collaborative Leadership Make a Difference for School Improvement?" *Educational Management Administration & Leadership*, 38, no. 6 (2010): 654–678.

Chapter 3

You Are Contagious . . . for Better or Worse

EXPECT TO LEARN

In this chapter, you will be introduced to research on stress, school leadership roles, and their connections. Additionally, proactive self-care measures will be reviewed. These strategies will become common themes as we dive into interviews and survey data in future chapters.

School leaders are expected to ensure strong outcomes for all students while nurturing an inclusive school culture. With instructional and transformational leadership's merger in the 2000s, the role has grown more complex than ever. Through external accountability and a dizzying array of mandates governing everything from social interactions to body mass indexes, school leaders are expected to exercise a style of leadership that creates a culture that promotes student achievement, student and staff well-being, and adherence to school policies.

Responsible for their own well-being and that of their school communities, school leaders are vulnerable to stressors embedded within the demands for effectiveness and efficiency.[1] School leaders face numerous job-related pressures that include increasing complexity in face of rising expectations, a sense of alienation and loneliness on the job, and the competing demands for roles and resources.

School leaders are often in reactive mode; this fact is central to the stress they experience. Regardless of the source, most potential stressors are unpredictable, uncontrollable, or both. Stress, as an experienced emotional response, typically involves reaction to dynamics either outside of our control or those that we perceive as potentially beyond our capacity to control. School leaders, especially principals at the center of children's lives, are uniquely vulnerable. Students come to school daily having lived most of their life experience outside of the school's influence. Students are in school for only seven hours a day; therefore, they spent the majority of their time in their homes, communities, and within wider social influences.

School leaders are constantly reacting to shifting dynamics of which they exercise influence, but little direct control. This task-oriented and interpersonal stress results from conflict with others or working to meet others' demands and expectations.[2] Furthermore, school leaders exert high levels of emotional labor to meet the daily challenges inherent to these reactive stances. Moreover, performing emotional labor can be difficult and can contribute to stress and burnout.[3]

Specific themes emerge in the literature that not only help frame the issues but also identify possible solutions to put into practice. It is important to note, however, that accepting more stress is the agreement a school leader makes with herself of himself upon accepting such a position. The transition from teacher to administrator involves accepting higher levels of task-related and interpersonal stress. Both roles contain stressors, of course. But when one transitions from an individual contributor to a managerial role, they are suddenly responsible for many more dynamics outside of their immediate control. They are called upon to intervene in interpersonal disputes that were once not on their radar between colleagues or between parents and teachers, for just one example.

The transition from teacher to administrator is challenging in this environment. Later, we will discuss administrator preparation programs and how they may better equip prospective leaders for this transition. Accepting higher levels of stress, however, is part of the transition from individual contributor to manager. Before diving into school leadership, individuals should examine their own perceptions and realities; in fact, the school leaders interviewed strongly recommend that prospective leaders understand their "why" before embarking on their leadership journey.

Several studies have analyzed school leadership stress. Long hours are at the top of the list. In one study, upward of 90% of school administrators reported working over sixty-two hours a week.[4] Caring for a school community not only involves being present when students and staff are in school but also involves leading from the front at school concerts and plays, being present at community events such as PTA meetings, and being responsive to "off-hours" dynamics such as bullying complaints and social media concerns.

Within that sixty-two-hour framework, it is unclear whether around-the-clock e-mail maintenance, Board of Education meeting attendance, and other work-related dynamics were included. The demand of always "being on" not only cuts into leisure time; it can often rob school leaders of being attentive to family concerns. As we will explore later, this can have significant consequences for school leaders with young families and female school leaders, in particular.

Further stressors identified in the literature include diminished revenues, insufficient time, paperwork overload, constant interruptions, email correspondence, and overall work-life balance struggles.[5] Similarly, a study of fifty-two school principals identified the following as major stressors: unpleasant relationships and people conflicts (identified by 100% of the study's participants as a major stressor), time constraints and related issues, school crises, overwhelming mandates, budgetary constraints, and fear of failure, among others.[6] In addition, more than 92% of those who responded claimed their biggest source of stress regarding people involved personal conflicts among teachers and between teachers and the principal. As one study participant stated, "It's interesting to note that adults don't get over conflicts easily like children do."[7] As schooling is a human-intensive endeavor, it is unsurprising that people conflicts rank high on school leader's stressor list.

Moreover, research identified external accountability mandates and sanctions as positively correlated with principal job stress, turnover rates, and transfer rates.[8] Although little direct evidence exists that the current accountability systems change school leadership behaviors, these systems can negatively influence working conditions and lead to higher turnover and transfer rates.

These stressors do not discriminate among beginning and veteran principals, rural and urban principals, male and female school leaders, and so on. There is evidence that female school leaders and those serving urban schools with high poverty levels are more vulnerable than others. Some researchers have begun to identify the principalship, in particular, as potentially a "job too big for one."[9]

As we have seen historically, however, the role "principal teacher" and later "principal," among other more specialized school leadership roles that have emerged, have remained stable over time. While mandates and their related stressors have increased, the idea that school leaders are responsible for their organization's health, success, and state test scores has continued. If anything, these expectations have increased over time. How, then are school leaders to promote their own personal and professional wellness while simultaneously carrying their school's success on their backs?

PROACTIVE SELF-CARE RESEARCH

School leader's daily work makes them vulnerable to several stressors that can have a negative impact on their own personal and professional leadership and their school community's overall health. It is important, therefore, to identify specific approaches and strategies that may help mitigate these potential negative effects. Furthermore, as will be discussed, it appears more important than ever that these conversations begin in preservice school leadership programs as teachers and service providers consider whether to pursue a school leadership career.

It is important to note that success as a classroom teacher often does not translate into success as a school leader, for several reasons that we will explore. Specific strategies to build and promote resiliency are vital for beginning and veteran administrators to consider as their work only grows in complexity in time and space. There is no escaping that the daily work will bring high stress levels; there may be specific leadership approaches and strategies to build resiliency in the face of those stressors.

Leading oneself is crucial to leading others. In one study, 96% of principals claimed to have experienced work-related stress at a level they believed was affecting their work habits, productivity, mental and physical health, and social life.[10] Gearing up, day after day, for high stress levels has a negative impact on both personal health and the overall school community's well-being. It should be noted that higher-than-usual stress levels are part and parcel of school leadership work.

Being responsible for an entire school's well-being, compared to that of an individual classroom, will inherently be a more stressful experience. Surfacing this reality in preparation programs and with practicing administrators is important. Successfully building these skills is an inside-out process. First, school leaders should identify the particular stressors that impact their personal and professional leadership. Then, in conjunction with strong mentor programs, they should reflect upon their leadership practices to identify which approaches and strategies may mitigate these negative experiences.

Although leadership starts with oneself, school leaders are also responsible for their larger school community's well-being. Research has identified several strategies and approaches that may be learned to help school leaders be more effective. Leaders have a major emotional impact on their wider communities. Labeled "emotional contagion," this concept posits that a school leader's emotional health will shape that of their school community's.[11]

Emotional contagion occurs when individuals reciprocate the emotions that they observe in those around them. As employees experience routine and novel events, leaders may shape their emotions through this process. It is important for school leaders to monitor their emotions and the impacts they may be having on those around them. The school leader can be a positive or negative source of emotions at work, with significant impacts on the daily teaching and learning that occurs within the schoolhouse.

Exploring emotional contagion and its impact also leads to discussions of specific leadership styles. Research has identified transformational leadership practices as positively correlated with higher relational, motivational, and emotional leadership outcomes. As Bass (1998) and his colleagues have demonstrated, transformational leaders appeal to their subordinate's developmental needs. They consider their emotional well-being and look to provide necessary supports for those who need them.

Most importantly, they explicitly build their staff's individual and collective self-efficacy. Self-efficacy represents an individual's perception of possessing the skills and capacity to succeed in a given situation. It promotes the idea of being "good enough" to overcome challenges. Appealing to their staff's emotions, building self-efficacy, and reframing stressful situations as growth opportunities all appear as transformational leadership practices. School leaders have the potential to be either a buffer against work stressors or a major source of stress for their subordinates.

Specific leadership approaches, strategies, and practices that promote self-efficacy among individual staff and collective entities as a whole can be taught and learned. One can imagine a powerful process whereby individual teachers, for example, build their individual capacity with a new literacy approach, and then over time, work collaboratively with their team to build a collective sense of efficacy. The school leader has an essential role to play in this process and outcomes of that process have powerful implications for the leader's stress level and well-being.

In the pages that follow, we will explore real-life experiences of beginning and veteran school leaders as they experience their role's occupational stress. Essential to this conversation are two dynamics: how school leaders build resiliency within themselves to meet these daily challenges and how they work with their school communities to build individual and collective self-efficacy.

NOTES

1. Caryn Wells and Barbara Klocko, "Can Teacher Leadership Reduce Principal Stress?" *Journal of School Leadership*, 25, no. 2 (2015): 315–317.

2. P. D. Harms, Marcus Crede, Michael Tynan, Matthew Leon, and Wonho Jeung, "Leadership and Stress: A Meta-analytic Review," *The Leadership Quarterly*, 28 (2017): 178–180.

3. Ronald Humphrey, "How Do Leaders Use Emotional Labor?" *Journal of Organizational Behavior*, 33, no. 5 (2012): 740–744.

4. L. Trenberth and P. Dewe, "An Exploration of the Role of Leisure in Coping with Work Related Stress using Sequential Stress Analysis," *British Journal of Guidance and Counseling*, 33, no. 1 (2015): 101–116.

5. Wells and Klocko, "Can Teacher Leadership Reduce Principal Stress?," 322–324.

6. Olusegun Agboola Sogunro, "Stress in School Administration: Coping Tips for Principals," *Journal of School Leadership*, 22, no. 3 (2012): 664–700.

7. Sogunro, "Stress in School Administration: Coping Tips for Principals," 674–676.

8. Hajime Mitani, "Principals' Working Conditions, Job Stress, and Turnover Behaviors Under NCLB Accountability Pressures," *Educational Administration Quarterly*, 54, no. 5 (2018): 822–862.

9. Wells and Klocko, "Can Teacher Leadership Reduce Principal Stress?," 329–333.

10. Sogunro, "Stress in School Administration: Coping Tips for Principals," 674–676.

11. Joseph B. Lyons and Tamara Schneider, "The Effects of Leadership Style on Stress Outcomes," *The Leadership Quarterly*, 20, no. 5 (2009): 737–748.

Chapter 4

Without This, Schools Cannot Move Forward

Building Trusting Relationships

EXPECT TO LEARN

With this chapter, we dive into our interview data to uncover common themes among several school leaders. Whether through a leadership transition or many years in the same role, school leaders discussed the importance of building trusting relationships to move their organizations forward, foster connections, and serve their communities.

All school leaders would state that they seek to build trusting relationships with students, staff, and the broader community. Wishing for trust to appear, however, is not enough to construct authentic relationships focused on the greater good. Instead, intentional approaches and strategies are necessary for school leaders to gradually build trust among their teams. Building trusting relationships is a lot like trying to lose weight; there are multiple steps involved. It is not enough just to exercise. Healthy habits and lifestyle choices are also required. In a similar manner, building trusting relationships requires that administrators employ several strategies simultaneously.

This chapter will focus on how school leaders can build trusting relationships with staff and the broader school community. Often, building trust with one group reinforces trust with the other. If a staff trusts their leader, they are more likely to feel supported in efforts to move the building or district forward. Likewise, when parents have trust in their school's leader, they are more likely to support efforts on behalf of staff even when it involves challenging conversations.

As a veteran school leader, Ryan has more than a decade of building-level leadership experience. This isn't much that he has not experienced over that time, which has been spent at the high school, middle school, and elementary level. Ryan was able to speak from experience about the double-edged sword often involved in trying to build trusting relationships.

> To be trusting, you have to trust others. Trust is a stressor from my experience. You want to trust people, but not everyone wants true feedback. People don't always have true motives, and that can be stressful.

To enter into trusting relationships involves being vulnerable enough to invest yourself in someone else's development. It means forming a mutually beneficial relationship where all parties are empowered by the other to grow, learn, and pursue goals. As Ryan highlights, there are times when school leaders can get burned by trusting people. The key is not to become cynical when that inevitably happens. Rather, trusting the larger picture and continuing to invest in others is the key.

Research on leadership and trust demonstrates that leaders can undertake specific behaviors and attitudes that promote trust among constituents. Dirks and Ferrin[1] reviewed the literature on transformational leadership and found that a leader's character is important because it informs how others perceive other characteristics such as dignity, integrity, dependability, and fairness. The authors found that leadership is directly related to several other important variables, including another's commitment to stretch themselves beyond their job description's narrow confines.

These "discretionary behaviors," called Organizational Citizenship Behaviors (OCBs), are less connected to job performance and more related to how much trust exists in a leader.[2] Putting into place a new student management process that requires staff to "think outside the box" will be directly related to how much staff trust their leader.

Trust is a complex concept and researchers often disagree on "how much" trust is needed in a leader for constituent to take risks outside their comfort zone. It is clear, however, that for any leader-led change initiative to be successful, staff must have some level of trust that their leader is dependable and has integrity.

Several school leaders that were interviewed gave specific approaches for developing trusting relationships with staff. Their feedback aligned closely with Dirks and Ferrin's findings that high levels of trust build commitment beyond a job's minimum competencies. As a new high school principal in a new district, Thomas understood that he had to quickly build relationships with students and staff. Talking less and listening more was an intentional part of Thomas's entry plan.

> It involved stepping back, observing, watching—it's hard to know what to change when you haven't lived it. My Assistant Principal came up through this

school, so I am also leaning on him to help me understand the culture. Some are apprehensive about me being an outsider—he came from a bigger district, is he going to want us to be like them? Some are, but I encourage them to ask me questions.

As Thomas discussed, honoring the existing culture is an essential element when building trust. As an outsider, it can be tempting to seek out a culture's faults and try to change them to a perceived better state. Chances are, however, that those within the building or district had major roles in developing that culture. As part of his entry strategy, Thomas focused on getting to know the students as part of learning the culture.

Getting to know the kids has been the best part. During the school day, I'm not really ever in my office. If you call me during that time, you will probably get my voicemail. I enjoy seeing the kids and staff, having 10-15 second conversations about "how's your day?" and constantly smiling. I want them to see a different role model—I'm an average guy and have a position where I can help people.

While deeper interactions also exist, Thomas has learned that getting around the building, being consistently visible, and prioritizing relationships with students go a long way toward building trust.

Madison also outlined a specific strategy for leveraging initial relationships to build trust with her large building. In any hiring process, there is a subset of building staff who participate in the actual interviews. These are usually key players within the building and are chosen due to their respect and influence. Madison has worked to utilize those on her interview committee as an "entrance team" to help her learn the building's culture and build trust.

In a past district, I learned to use the interview team as your initial planning team. These people already have something invested in you. They had to come back to the building and tell the staff "this was the one, this was the best candidate." So they are already walking with you and are in a great position to help with building those trusting relationships.

In Madison's building, this entry team met once per month for her first year on the job. She was able to leverage their deep knowledge of the community to help assess the building's needs and make informed decisions. This is a strategy that can be employed in any hiring situation that involves an interview committee.

While most transitions involve school leaders entering a new building or district and having to quickly learn the culture, Avery's transition was more unique. She was hired as a new assistant principal in the same middle school where she taught for over a decade. Her transition was not so much learning a new culture but changing roles from contributor to leader.

> There are pros and cons. It's a unique situation, you know people and they know you, the good, bad, and the ugly. I experienced the culture from the teacher side and now on the administrative side. I think it's been a strength. I can be a sounding board for what we are doing and why.

Avery spoke about leading a sixth-grade team-teaching initiative that had been discussed among her teacher colleagues for many years. Because she knew the lay of the land, she was able to lead a significant change in her first year as assistant principal. Without her background knowledge and trusting relationships, this would not have been possible.

Pros and cons to this situation exist. Although she had immediate trust with many of her staff members, she also found that some former colleagues had unrealistic expectations for their relationship. Without that fresh start that often comes with changing districts, there is potential for some staff to have role confusion.

> I'm not considered top-down yet, so people have felt maybe too comfortable coming to me with things. I want to be someone who can give rationale, but staff need to understand that part of my job now is to move these initiatives forward even if every last person isn't in full agreement all of the time.

In her new role, Avery already knows her student's names and has worked directly with most of the staff. Her challenge is different than Thomas's or Madison's. Instead of coming into a new district having to quickly get up to speed, Avery's challenge was to leverage her trusting relationships in her new role. With an early success under her belt and a sound perspective on how to navigate other's expectations, Avery has entered her new role in a strong position.

Whether entering a new environment or navigating a familiar one in a new role, the administrators interviewed described intentional efforts to build shared leadership among their staffs. Building shared leadership has been demonstrated as essential to developing high-functioning teams. As one study[3] discusses, constructing shared leadership among a diverse staff, such as a large building faculty, can lead to performance improvements.

Shared development structures can help improve results in two major ways. First, when leadership is shared among a group and distributed to those outside of the formal authority structure, group motivation increases and leads to better outcomes. Group trust increases and is an important predictor of group success.[4] As more and more individuals participate on building- and district-level teams and are recognized for their expertise, individuals have more opportunities to interact with one another and therefore form trusting bonds. This dynamic increases the overall knowledge pool that individuals within the group recognize and can lead to better group decisions.

Closely related to increased trust among the group is another shared leadership outcome. When individuals trust one another to greater degrees, they spend less time monitoring each other's behaviors and more time focused on work activities.[5] For schools, this means that teams spend less time gossiping about one another and more time focused on serving students and the school community. As teachers in a building recognize each other's expertise and participate in a collaborative teaming process, their trust levels for each other increase. Teachers who work together and trust one another are more likely to produce positive outcomes for students.

The school leaders interviewed for this study demonstrated their awareness for creating shared leadership and building trusting relationships. Often, these relationships develop as building and district leaders spend more time within their current roles. Greg is in his second go-around as principal in his elementary school. He served for five years, left for a district-level position in another district, and decided to return when he discovered he missed his old position. Greg was candid about how his longevity has helped build trust with staff.

> There's something to be said for staying in one place and building that culture of trust. At night, I can come home and even if I wasn't perfect that day, I know that my staff has grace with me, my parents have grace with me, and I can make that better.

Consistent with research on shared leadership, Greg outlines that his trusting relationships built among staff have paid off. Rather than worrying about the mistakes he made at night, he can focus on his family and preparing for the next day knowing that his staff and community trust him. That level of trust cannot happen during a transition period; it is built over time through consistent and dependable interactions.

> I can manage this because of those relationships that I've built. I don't lead top-down. It's silly things, like knowing when a staff member's kid is sick. I hurt my foot two weeks ago and staff were texting me asking if I was okay. I know we're not best friends, but there is a culture here of not being on your own.

In a profession often marked by loneliness, building trusting relationships is a prime strategy to build shared leadership and increase everyone's level of care. Greg hits the nail on the head: principals' staff are not their best friends and difficult conversations sometimes have to happen, but a shared level of trust breaks down personal barriers. When a staff demonstrates that level of care toward one another, they most likely also show that level of care toward their students.

Developing trusting relationships with staff is primary for prospective and practicing school leaders. Trust with staff can often translate to trust with the larger community as well. Several of the same characteristics—dependability, empathic listening, visibility, and others—relate not only to relationships with staff but also with parents and the broader school community.

Relationships with parents are often ranked among the most stressful dynamics for school leaders, especially at the building level. The survey data also reflected this trend. When asked to list their top five stressors, the word "parent" showed up as the number one response. Although the way it was worded often varied, it is clear that working directly with challenging parents is among school leadership's most stressful undertakings.

Among building-level respondents, difficult parent interactions were consistently the top-ranked stressors. Interestingly, this data differed among tenured and nontenured building-level leaders. Consistent with the overall trend, "parents" was reflected in nearly one in three (30%) of all tenured principal or assistant principal responses as their top-ranked stressor. Among those nontenured building-level respondents, "parents" showed up in only 12% of the top-ranked stressors and was the third-most popular top choice.

One explanation may be the respondent pool. Among survey respondents who hold tenure, the vast majority were building principals rather than assistant principals. For those nontenured respondents, the split among principals and assistant principal was even (50% in each category for nontenured respondents). It could be that parent interactions among principals are, on average, more stressful than those among assistant principals. Legally, for example, principals are the only building-level administrator who can suspend a student. Often, principals also serve as the school's bullying prevention coordinator. Principals may be involved in more progressively punitive interactions with parents than assistant principals. The most severe issues in a school often land on the principal's desk.

Several administrators outlined strategies that may help mitigate these challenging parent conversations and build trust before difficult interactions take place. As a new principal in a new community, Tony was hired on July 1 and took advantage of the summer months to help build these relationships while putting many miles on his vehicle.

> I started over the summer and tried to interact with as many staff and families as possible. I visited a lot of houses that summer, especially those that when I

pulled data showed some struggles academically or behaviorally. I tried to get parents on my side right off the bat. Many of them have had negative school experiences and you have to show them who you are.

Tony hit on a factual statement as it relates to difficult parent conversations. Many "difficult" parents, who get labeled as such, often had very negative school experiences when they were students. Their only lens through which to view the school system is negative. They may have struggled in school or felt that they were treated unfairly. A positive initial interaction, preferably face to face, can help establish a trusting relationship before any more challenging conversations have to take place.

Similar to Tony's strategy to visit as many families as possible, Richard prefers early contact with families to build trust. In his district-level role as a special education chairperson, Richard is often at the mercy of several dynamics which he cannot directly control. When a student moves into his district in need of a special education placement, Richard has to consider budgetary items, transportation requirements, placement considerations, among others. Although he cannot directly control any of these, he has found success with proactive and open communication.

> I try to contact the parent as soon as possible, even just to introduce myself and let people know that I'm on it. I've found that those early phone calls buy you flexibility and trust. It tells the parent that you may not know the exact answer right now, but that you're on it. Keeping them informed at each step of the process is very important.

Richard employs this strategy not only with families but also with the multiple stakeholders required to successfully place a student. Working with individual building principals, school psychologists, transportation directors, business executives, and others also requires proactive and open communication. Building trust among the team and communicating openly with everyone involved has been a successful strategy for Richard.

> Using the human resources that you have at your disposal is important. Don't take everything on yourself. Use the people around you and their expertise to help make decisions. Don't try to make every decision yourself because there are pieces to the puzzle that you don't have.

Over time, these consistent and dependable interactions build trust among all stakeholders involved and make it more likely that even the most challenging situations find a successful outcome. Making early phone calls, even before a situation is fully resolved, is among the most important strategies for building this trust. For building-level leaders, this could look like a phone call home immediately after a playground incident. Although an investigation still has to take place, an early phone call home conveys that the school leader is reliable and committed to a positive resolution. Richard's example of keeping multiple stakeholders informed for special education placements throughout the process is an excellent district-level example.

When looking to build trust, it is important to recognize which skill sets move teams in a positive direction and which detract from it. If the goal is to build trust and shared leadership among a teaching staff, for example, principals and assistant principals need to consider other's ideas far more than their own. Often, their own idea, if formed in their prior district or position, may not be well-received by those who have lived in the current culture for years. As a veteran administration, Ryan was very aware of this dynamic when he inherited his current building. Lessons learned over a career can help inform these strategies.

> Your job is to grow people and listen to people. Early in my career, I made the mistake of trying to show people how much I knew. Now, I'm at the point where I'm older than my Superintendent. I've been around. I'm the second oldest administrator that we have on staff.

Ryan has personal and professional history behind him to help inform his entry plan into a new building. To empower others, their ideas have to shine and they have to have ownership over the outcomes. An idea arrived at collaboratively, even if it is not exactly what the administrator would have envisioned, is better than an imposed outcome arrived at without staff input.

In many ways, the skill set needed to build trusting relationships is that of school counselor rather than manager or administrator. School counselors are tasked with listening deeply to student concerns and helping them reflect in ways that benefit their mental and physical well-being. Many newer student management philosophies, such as restorative practices, are centered on this concept. Rather than condemn and punish behavior, these strategies seek to understand the behavior's root causes and put interventions into place to benefit the student.

As a first-year assistant principal, Monica has been busy building those relationships. She has been so successful that some of her students do not realize that she is an administrator when they are called to her office. She told the story of being mistaken for a counselor during a recent night out.

> I was out to dinner with my husband one night and a student came up to me and said, "Hi, I think you're my counselor?" I think a lot of students see me that way because of our interactions. I spend a lot of time working on mental

health issues with students, and I think they see me more that way than they do an administrator or disciplinarian.

We know that putting students into detention over and over again does very little to change behavior. Listening to instead of lecturing at people is a valuable skill set when building trust among students and staff alike.

One of education's benefits as a career is that each school year brings a renewal and fresh energy to the profession. Students and staff arrive back in September ready to dive into the school year with gusto. Maintaining that energy level throughout the long academic year can be a challenge, especially for school leaders who face daily challenges and difficult conversations.

Even in her first year as assistant principal, Avery has discovered that bringing a fresh perspective and renewed mindset to each day helps build trusting relationships. The first year can be challenging as the job's realities rear themselves in a way that they do not during an internship. A positive outlook every day can certainly help.

> I try to treat every day like it's a new day. Saying good morning to each student, every parent and adult, and I have found that the more high fives I give, the more I get back. It just seems to propel the day. Smile more, ask them how's your day? I have to let them know that it's not horrible.

Each school day is a new opportunity to building trusting relationships with students, staff, and the greater school community. Daily, dependable, and consistent interactions are the motor oil that fuel the trusting engines. In handling challenging students, staff, and parents, starting with early phone calls and listening rather than lecturing are two strategies that the administrators interviewed have found successful.

CHAPTER SUMMARY

Whether new to a building or fostering changes as a veteran leader, building trusting relationships is essential to any effort. As the school leaders interviewed suggest and the survey data confirms, getting to know staff on a personal level breaks down barriers and promotes strong relationships. Staff will follow leaders who they believe know and value them. It is often those small, mundane, seemingly boring interactions that build trust over time. Leaders who focus on building these relationships have a much better chance of moving their communities forward than those who do not.

NOTES

1. Kurt T. Dirks and Donald Ferrin, "Trust in Leadership: Meta-Analytic Findings and Implications for Research and Practice," *Journal of Applied Psychology*, 87, no. 4 (2012): 611–615.

2. Dirks and Ferrin, "Trust in Leadership: Meta-Analytic Findings and Implications for Research and Practice," 615–617.

3. Marcus Drescher, Isabell Welpe, M. Aubrey Korsgaard, Arnold Picot, and Rolf Wigard, "The Dynamics of Shared Leadership: Building Trust and Enhancing Performance," *Journal of Applied Psychology*, 99, no. 5 (2014): 771–772.

4. Drescher et al., "The Dynamics of Shared Leadership: Building Trust and Enhancing Performance," 773.

5. Drescher et al., "The Dynamics of Shared Leadership: Building Trust and Enhancing Performance," 774.

Chapter 5

Making It All Fit

Professional Fit and Work-Life Balance

EXPECT TO LEARN

In this chapter, interviewees and survey respondents share their insight into how their work and home lives fit together. Honest reflection and conversations with family are crucial to this. Often it is better to persist in a current position that fits into lifestyle for a little longer than to jump to a higher-profile position too soon that puts work-life balance out of alignment. Moreover, differences emerged among responses for female and male administrators.

"Set the stage of who you are and you can be true to yourself. Don't sell lies during the interview process." Fresh off his degree program, Tony was interviewing for his first principal position in a rural school district thirty minutes from his home. With working spouse and a young child at home, Tony understood that pursuing a principal position would entail changes to his and his family's daily routines.

Moreover, Tony did not bring a wealth of experience to his interview. He taught middle school for eight years and was hired within his same district as a dean of students during his administrative program. Although he earned a solid reputation within a short period of time, he was not long on official leadership experience. His first principalship in a community over thirty minutes from home would require a high level of reflection within himself and his staff.

As Tony's story illustrates, it is important for school leaders to be reflective about their career path, where they envision finishing their career, and how their career journey fits within their broader family context. Understanding professional fit and its connection to work-life balance is crucial. They are two sides of the same coin. Finding the right fit—when the job is surrounded by professional and personal supports that promote work-life balance—is more important than blindly climbing a career ladder.

Successful school leaders will find that opportunities continuously present themselves. Rather than jumping at the next rung in the ladder and the next pay increase, school leaders should be reflective about how their current or any future positions fit within their specific life situation.

Tony's story, in that case, seems counterintuitive. He found himself pursuing opportunities in other communities with a young family at home. In discussing this particular opportunity with his wife, however, he decided to go for it.

> My wife was totally supportive. She teaches 30 minutes away as well, and we had to have that conversation. When I said I wanted to do this, she was 100% supportive. I wouldn't have done it if we both weren't on board.

Staying late for Board meetings, attending his student's sporting events, and other job-related functions are possible because Tony and his spouse decided that the position fit their personal and professional lives. Tony was honest with himself and his family when it came to the pressures his new job would entail, but having his family on board was a key factor in pursuing and accepting his first principal position.

Part of reflecting upon professional fit and work-life balance is realizing that everyone will have a different story and a different set of pressures. While a principalship fit Tony's lifestyle, other school leaders may find themselves in different places. Vanessa was a veteran building leader who had spent several years as an assistant principal and was in her third year in a principal position. She had earned the opportunity to lead a building and was succeeding in the role. It became apparent, however, that having young children and a working spouse while leading a building was taking a toll.

When a district-level position arose in a neighboring district, she decided to pursue it. After nine years at the building level, Vanessa felt pulled toward trying something new at a time when her family responsibilities were growing.

> After nine years, I had the itch to do something different. My weekends weren't mine. I don't mind spending three hours in the office on Saturdays, but it became a lot harder with two young kids. I wanted to at least explore this position.

Vanessa interviewed for the district-level position in another school community and was hired. After seventeen years in the same district overall and nine years as a building-level administrator, she felt pulled in a new direction as her idea of professional fit changed. While she missed being directly responsible for students as a principal, she reflected upon how her new position fit within her home life.

> My home time is my home time now. I can also do some professional development that wasn't possible when you are being pulled in every possible direction all day. As a principal, so many people reach out to you, you walk away, come back, and you have 50 new emails and they are all important. Now, I can usually get my work done within the context of my day.

What worked for Vanessa ten years ago no longer worked. Vanessa was also reflective about the fact that not everyone understood her decision. The building she led had undergone significant leadership transition in the past ten years and she was only on her second full year. Her staff, as one can imagine, did not want to see her leave. School leaders should understand that not everyone will be supportive of the choices that have to be made when being reflective about professional fit and work-life balance.

Family dynamics and prioritizing the most important relationships are one aspect when reflecting upon this idea. Supervisory support—or lack thereof—in an administrative position is another. Significant stress can result when school leaders find themselves in situations where their supervisors demonstrate weak leadership. This is especially true at the building level when so many decisions are made in the district office. Whether it is seeking a new position or when district office turnover occurs within the same district, a lack of support from above can help or hinder professional fit.

Ryan is a veteran building principal who has served in several positions within the same district over the past decade. When he arrived at his new district, however, he was not sure the professional fit was there.

> It's hard when you don't trust your Superintendent. I came from a school where everyone did. And then I came here, and it was different. I wasn't ready for it at first and I made some mistakes. Some were real, and some were silly. I remember going to my first administrative meeting here and sitting at a table. The Superintendent said to me "this is a central office table, not an assistant principal table." I thought, wow.

Luckily for Ryan, that superintendent soon retired and a new superintendent was hired who built a very different, and more supportive, culture. Tony's story is also illustrative here. As a brand-new principal in a different school community, potential existed that he would feel like an outsider. However, the exact opposite happened because everyone was new to their positions.

> Part of what made the fit strong for me is that everyone is new. Everyone. the Superintendent, all principals except one. The culture is that no one has to feel stupid asking questions and opening up to each other because everyone has a bunch of questions, and the Superintendent encourages us to understand that we aren't going to have every answer.

Had Tony's first principalship been in a position such that he was the only "new kid on the block," he may have felt differently about the professional fit. Rather, he was new to his position on a team where everyone was new to their positions. Being vulnerable and reaching out for help is much easier when a supportive culture exists.

Professional fit is maximized when family needs merge with a supportive school culture. Monica had just finished her school leadership program and was scanning assistant principal positions for the right fit. She found it in an eleven-month administrative position in a medium-sized school district where several administrators also had young children.

> Becoming a mom put everything back into priority for me. When I interviewed here, they told me I could bring my daughter to evening events. It also helps that the principal has young children and often does that too. Although there are stressful days, I never feel like I have to choose between being a mom and an assistant principal.

Monica was also selective about which job to take as she had multiple opportunities. While higher-paying or more "prestigious" titles were possibilities, she opted for an eleven-month position where she would have snow days and school breaks free to be with her family. Her first administrative position was exactly where she felt she needed to be at this point in her family life. In the future, Monica acknowledges she may pursue principalships or district-level positions but would not trade the fit her current position holds at this point in her life.

The worst thing a school leader can do is jump to a new opportunity for the wrong reasons. Having honest conversations with loved ones and reflecting upon priorities are crucial when school leaders consider new opportunities or reconsider their current positions. At the end of the day, a school leader's family life is more important than climbing the career ladder too rapidly into higher-paying or more prestigious positions. This is especially true for school leaders who have younger children at home.

When speaking with a diverse mix of administrators across gender, family situation, experience level, and school setting, a contrast emerged between principalships and district-level positions. Several administrators, many of them females with younger families, reported that they pursued district-level positions because the professional fit was better for promoting work-life balance.

The survey data supports the trend that school leaders may perceive district-level positions more flexible for balancing work and home than principal positions. Moreover, the survey data also suggests that female administrators may seek district-level positions more than principalships due to this perception.

The survey data sought to uncover trends among school leaders for their happiness levels, stress levels, and work-life balance challenges. Among principals, 60% of respondents identified as male with 92% of all principals reporting their status as married. By contrast, among district-level respondents, 63% of respondents were female with only 75% of all district-level administrators reporting their status as married. Within both groups, approximately 50% of respondents reported having at least one child under thirteen years of age at home. Moreover, within both groups, approximately 85% of respondents were within thirty-five to fifty-four years of age.

Although perhaps not statistically significant, slightly higher percentages of district-level administrators (87%) reported being "high or moderately satisfied" with their job than those in principal positions (82%). Perhaps significantly, a substantially higher number of district-level administrators (34%) reported being in their current role between four and six years than those in principal positions (16%). The four- to six-year mark for any administrative position may be a significant marker for job satisfaction. By year four, tenure decisions have to be made in many states.

In addition, if a school leader is successful in their current position, by year six, they may have had feelers for other administrative positions at a higher pay or prestige level. Persisting in the same administrative position between four and six years was a major difference in the data set between principals and district-level administrators.

Both the administrative interviews and the surveys demonstrated a perceived difference between principalships and district-level positions for professional fit and the ability to balance work and home. While limited in scope, these results would be important for prospective and practicing administrators to consider as they scan open positions. There are times when administrators, despite their success, have accomplished all they believe they can at the building level, as in Vanessa's case.

In other instances, as we saw with Greg in our opening vignette, returning to the building level after a brief foray into district-level work can provide enhanced professional focus. The key is to have honest and reflective conversations with one's family and understand that its often best to pursue the right fit than to climb an administrative ladder for money and prestige.

Chapter 5

PURSUING WORK-LIFE BALANCE

Closely connected to professional fit is pursuing work-life balance. In many ways, the two are opposite sides of the same coin. School leaders who fit professionally into their positions should be able to implement strategies that promote a healthy balance between home and work.

Interestingly, many school leaders interviewed work in districts beyond their immediate home area. Tony, for example, is a first-year principal in a district thirty-five minutes from his home. Along with his young family and spouse, who is also a teacher thirty-five minutes away in a different district, this has the potential to throw off any semblance of work-life balance. Tony maintains a healthy balance by focusing on his own mental and physical well-being.

> I try to get to the gym before everyone in my house is up during the work week. Although it sounds like it wouldn't be this way, the drive is actually positive. By the time I walk in the door, I've processed all of the stuff that happened that day, and I'm ready to be a father and a husband.

Richard's story is very similar. As mentioned earlier, Richard transitioned to a district-level position due to its perceived flexibility versus a building principalship. The latter position, ironically, was a much shorter drive to his home than the district-level position he sought. However, Richard has found that the distance has helped him develop habits that support the longer commute.

> The longer drive actually forces me to be more intentional about my morning routine than if I was only 10 minutes away. I can square away thoughts in the car and emails when I get to work at about 6:30 am. Then I am ready for the day.

While some administrators like to get out of the house early and into the office, others develop a home-office routine that meets their needs. Thomas spent twenty-two years as a teacher and assistant principal in one district before pursuing his first principal position in a neighboring district about twenty-five minutes away. To promote work-life balance and create boundaries between the office and the living room, Thomas has established his own routine.

> I have a great home office situation. I can get up early and get some work done; sit on the couch and answer emails if I need to. Then, I can prioritize what needs to be done on campus. My staff also knows that my routine is to clean up emails before the day starts and everyone gets into the office, including myself. So they

know they can email me after hours, and I will see it before the next day starts and whatever needs to be addressed.

Tony, Richard, and Thomas expressed a common refrain among the school leaders that were interviewed: a desire to "clean up" the previous day's issues to the best of their ability before the next day starts. While Tony and Richard like to get of the house early and address those concerns, Greg likes to remain home longer in a home office and accomplish the same goal. Each school leader can learn from others but ultimately develop their own morning routines.

Two female school leaders interviewed brought a different perspective to this topic. While many male school leaders talked about intentionally separating work and home into different spheres, Avery and Monica spoke about integrating their two worlds. Both have young children and are in their first administrative positions as secondary assistant principals.

Avery's first administrative opportunity came in the same district and building in which she taught for twelve years. Moreover, her own children attend the same school. Perhaps due to this, Avery had no choice but to seek strategies to integrate work and home. She reflected intensely on seeking the right balance between being at work and being at home when those lines are more blurred than bifurcated.

> How do you strike a balance between being passionate about work but also knowing that you need to shut it off? My own daughter is in this building. I fear that if my patience is pretty low at work, then when I get home it will be even lower. That is hard.

Despite this, Avery has found ways to integrate work and life. She has lived, worked, and raised children in the same community for her entire life. Unlike Tony, Richard, and Thomas, her commute between work and home can be counted in seconds, not minutes. That rootedness, however, has proven to be a strength for her as she begins her next career phase as an administrator.

> I have found ways to bring the two together. I coach softball outside of school, for example, so many of these students are my players. I get to know them in a different way and that helps. I'm a close community member so people know what I'm about. The teachers and families here already knew me when I took over this position.

As a known quantity, Avery did not have to spend time building trust that others may have. She had it already as a veteran teacher, community member, and parent within the same building. Moreover, she has found ways to blend her passion as a school leader and an engaged parent in the same school community.

Monica, moreover, has developed strategies to integrate work and home rather than intentionally create boundaries between them. As a young mother in her first administrative position, Monica knew that any career move would entail reflection about how to reconceptualize work and home. Fortunately, her position lends itself to fulfillment as a professional and an appropriate focus as a mother.

> Having a child while pursuing an administrative position at the same time forced me to reflect on how that was going to happen. However, in this position I can bring my daughter to evening events. People get to see me in that role, a similar role as a parent to what they may have. I think it has helped me build trust with staff and families.

Monica intentionally sought a position that would lend itself to integrating work and home. Evening events such as basketball games, talent shows, and musicals have become family events that she can share with her young daughter. While never a perfect arrangement every day or week, these strategies have helped Monica seek balance between work and home in different ways that others may pursue.

Clear distinctions developed during interviews among men and women as they discussed their strategies around work-life balance. While men tended to speak about creating intentional boundaries that protected home from work, and vice versa, women talked about pursuing approaches that integrated the two worlds. Administrative survey data also indicates that divisions exist among men and women in this area.

Survey data surrounding career duration, tenure status, and family situation demonstrated differences among men and women. Only 32% of men reported being in their current position between two and four years, while 50% of women reported the same. Interestingly, 50% of men reported being tenured in their current position versus only 36% of women reporting that they attained tenure status. Male administrators, both at the building and district levels, appear to jump to new positions at a higher rate while also persisting in positions longer.

Moreover, 90% of male respondents reported their status as married while only 84% of women reported the same. Additionally, 66% of male administrators reported having at least one child under age thirteen at home while only 39% of female school leaders concurred. In this survey set, male administrators appear more likely to be married with younger children at home while female school leaders, although married at high rates, tend to have either older children or no children at all.

Combined with interview data, these statistics point to differences in how men and women may perceive work-life balance. Importantly, it highlights that for females, school leadership may be a career path more desirable during mid-to-late career while more men pursue administration earlier in their careers. Marriage rates were not dissimilar; the main difference between men and women was young children in the household.

Interestingly, differences also existed among men and women when asked for their motivations for pursuing school leadership as a career path. Several choices were presented and respondents could choose all options they felt applied to their personal situation. While 50% of men responded that "increased pay" was a major motivator, only 33% of women reported the same. Moreover, 60% of men chose "exert more influence" as a motivating factor while only 42% of women chose this option.

If more men are pursuing school leadership while having younger children at home, seeking higher paid positions could be attractive. This factor could also help explain why more men appear to jump from position to position more frequently than the female respondents in the survey. Males, however, tended to report their status as tenured at a higher rate than females did.

Perhaps most importantly, male administrators reported that they are "highly satisfied" with their current roles at a higher rate than females. While nearly two-thirds (64%) of men expressed this, only half (50%) of women did the same. This could mean that male-centric strategies around separating work and home are more successful in promoting job satisfaction than attempting to integrate the two. More research into this topic would yield insight into what factors contribute to high job satisfaction among male and female administrators.

The survey also asked school leaders to reflect upon their high-leverage strategies for sustaining balance outside of work. Not surprisingly, maintaining physical exercise was the top response among both men and women. During interviews, men tended to talk openly about their early morning routines, which often included an exercise regimen, while women did not speak of this as intentionally. As with creating boundaries between work and home or integrating these worlds, it may be that men prefer physical wellness as something to check off of their lists while women incorporate into their workday.

Moreover, both men and women reported that spending time with family was a main strategy to maintain mental wellness. Further questioning may have brought interesting insight into whether male school leaders viewed this dynamic as separate from work as they reported while discussing boundary setting.

Additionally, the female school leaders interviewed were more likely to discuss integrating family time and work time in specific ways, such as bringing young children to evening school events. Regardless, both men and women reported physical exercise and spending time with family as their top two high-leverage strategies for maintaining a healthy perspective on work and home.

Throughout this chapter, differences among administrators were noted when discussing professional fit and work-life balance. For the former, divergent data existed between building-level and district-level administrators for how they perceived their roles and their fit into their professional and personal lives.

Moreover, men and women differed in their responses when discussing work-life balance issues. It is important for school leaders to reflect upon their unique life situations and have honest conversations with family about pursuing different administrative roles. No two roles are exactly the same; different districts have different cultures, expectations, senses of urgency, leadership structures, and demands. Thoughtful scanning, honest conversations, and self-reflection are all crucial ingredients while promoting professional fit and work-life balance in school leadership positions.

CHAPTER SUMMARY

Professional fit and work-life balance are crucial concepts for school leaders. When taken for granted, these leadership positions can negatively impact a leader's personal and family lives. Key takeaways from this chapter include the following:

- Be authentic during the interview process; don't sell lies.
- Honestly reflect with self and family before jumping to a new position.
- Develop personal and professional habits that promote healthy balance.
- Female and male leaders often view balance differently.

Chapter 6

Is It Lonely at the Top?

Navigating Leadership Isolation and Loneliness

EXPECT TO LEARN

In this chapter, we will explore how leadership positions may be isolating and lonely for school leaders. Especially at the building level, principals and assistant principals are often stuck between powerful central offices and their staffs. However, school leaders may suffer from objective isolation but have access to networks that those without power may not possess.

Any teacher who pursues administrative degrees or positions is likely to hear jokes about "going to the dark side." While most jabs are made in jest, there is some truth to any comment. Several factors have contributed to school leadership being viewed as "different" from the teaching profession over the years. The profession's culture, in addition, often pits administrators against teachers when student success remains the ultimate goal for both groups.

The principalship, in particular, can be the loneliest of all administrative positions for several reasons. First, principals are often the only person in their building with that specific job title. There are plenty of teachers, aides, clerical staff, and others. Some buildings even have multiple assistant principals. But for a building principal deciding on student suspension, for example, she or he knows they are the only person in that building with the legal authority to make such decisions.

Moreover, principals are often stuck between powerful central offices, where many of the big decisions involving curriculum, instruction, budget, and others are made, and their teaching staffs. While central offices possess a lot of power, principals are often closer on a day-to-day basis with their staffs. Decisions handed down from above often fall to principals to communicate, even though principals may not have been involved in the decision-making process at all.

Ryan has been a building-level leader for over a decade and has worked for multiple superintendents and central office directors. Whether as a principal or an assistant principal, Ryan has experienced this loneliness firsthand throughout his administrative career.

> It's very lonely at times, for sure. You're not central office. They are friendly, but they are not your friends. You're not one of the other people either. There isn't a peer group to vent to on a daily basis when stress or frustrating things happen.

Ryan described this in-between, middle-management dynamic from his own personal experience. One of the challenges that teachers face when they earn their first formal school leadership position is navigating this middle ground. An advantage of moving into a new district as an administrator is being able to maintain some of those teacher connections from the previous district. Administrators who move up the ranks within the district in which they taught may have a more challenging experience in this area.

As a principal, loneliness may be exacerbated if the position exists in a larger district with multiple buildings. Often, data displays will compare buildings across a district for numbers on attendance, test scores, reading levels, among others. Ryan has also experienced this dynamic in his many years at the building level.

> The worst is when the district office pits principals against one another. These are the people that are supposed to be on your team and you feel like you're in a competition against them. I think everyone is trying to survive a little bit.

Although each principal possesses some level of autonomy to lead their buildings, several factors may impact freedom. In smaller districts where one or more buildings, including the central office, exist on the same campus, a building principal may never gain that autonomy. The superintendent is always around, and depending on that relationship, it can be a positive or a negative. In larger districts more dispersed over a geographic area, it may be possible to earn some level of autonomy. Central office dynamics often play a major role in how much autonomy a principal feels that they truly possess.

Lacking a peer group on a daily basis is one reason why school leaders, especially at the building level, often feel lonely. Another is the very nature of their job. Administrators are handling sensitive and confidential information on an hour-by-hour basis. Rarely a day goes by without handling a confidential student situation or being involved with a personnel matter with an employee. These situations often require principals to have to make very quick decisions with the best information that they can, and they are often second-guessed. The job's confidential nature was discussed by several administrators throughout the interviews.

Madison spoke candidly about the loneliness that she feels when she handles confidential student information and cannot share with her staff. Often, staff want to know why certain decisions were made surrounding a student, and not being able to give them the full picture often leads to staff feeling frustrated. Madison always explains that there are items she cannot share due to their confidential nature, but this does not always satisfy all staff who want the full picture.

> Loneliness is really about the things that you can't share with staff. Family situations, personnel situations that involve other staff members, something coming down from the district office that is on the horizon but you've been told not to tell staff yet. Those are the biggest factors that make this job lonely at times.

Madison addressed both the middle-manager environment in which principals work and their constant need to make decisions around confidential information. Madison is the only principal in her 500-student and 75-staff member elementary school, and even though she has an assistant principal, the ultimate decisions on matters rest with her.

As a new assistant principal, Monica has experienced this loneliness early in her administrative career. Although she has a special education background and is used to handling confidential student information, her exposure has been taken to another level in her first administrative role. She also experienced, for the first time, staff members questioning why she was not as visible as they believed she ought to be.

> In the beginning of the year, I wasn't as visible in classrooms or hallways as I wanted to be. I would stand outside the main office during passing time, but teachers wouldn't see me. Teachers started to ask the principal why the assistants weren't visible. I get it, don't get me wrong, but it's not like I can tell them that I was dealing with the state troopers all day.

Meeting everyone's needs while handling highly sensitive and confidential student situations is challenging. This is especially true at the building level where, as we have seen, the principal is often the only administrator in their building. At the elementary level, in particular, this is often the case.

Interestingly, loneliness was not raised as a concern is any of the district-level leadership interviews. Several themes repeated themselves at the building and district levels, but loneliness was not one of them. While many building-level leaders cited the need for central office support for their professional success, none of the interviewed district-level leaders spoke of their principals in the same manner. District-level leaders did not speak poorly of their building leaders, but they also did not reference their jobs being dependent upon principals and assistant principals as directly.

Feeling isolated from or ambivalent toward central office staff can heighten feelings of isolation among principals and assistant principals. Building-level leaders are dependent upon the central office for budgetary considerations and human resource decisions. When principals feel supported by their central office, their feelings of isolation may decrease. Greg discussed his relationship with his central office in a large district.

> Over the years I've learned how important central office is to your life. They can make your job difficult, or they can make it more manageable. It depends on their support. You're going to have to make tough decisions, and when they will support you—that's huge. They can invest in your development.

Central office administrators, particularly the superintendent and any assistant superintendents, may also have control over career trajectories in ways that are not reciprocal. John is only in his fourth year as an administrator but has been in several buildings throughout his district. Although his movement is due to his strengths as a leader, the constant movement has also altered his career path. As a former high school teacher, he started off as a school leader at the secondary level, but quickly realized that his central office's plans can change. Now, John finds himself tasked with changing a culture in a large elementary school setting.

> I never anticipated being an elementary school principal. I was approached by our DO when I was a middle-school assistant principal, and went to our high school as an assistant for one year. Then, they changed their mind again, and I was moved to the elementary school to clean up "problems."

As demonstrated, building trusting relationships, fostering shared leadership, and learning a building's culture all take time. John has served in three school leadership positions in his four years as an administrator; moreover, he neither did apply for nor seek out any of these career moves. While they all occurred due to support from his central office, the constant movement can also hinder relationship-building efforts.

Furthermore, John's central office made it clear that they anticipated quick results from his most recent move to an elementary principalship. When discussing his biggest professional and personal stressors at work, the pressure to deliver quick results, while knowing that such results take time to accomplish, was at the forefront of John's mind.

The biggest stressor for me this year is leading that cultural change. It's not that it's not going well or can't happen, but it was made clear to me that is has to happen now. I was told, jokingly, "You have one year to fix this." I told them, "I'll get my resume ready." I'm joking, but it's serious. It wasn't an ultimatum, but there's something to that.

Although John's central office may not have intended to layer additional stress onto an already-charged environment, they did. A common theme among building-level interviews is the presence of central office in their lives. None of the central office administrators interviewed discussed their principals and assistant principals in a similar manner. It may be that central office administrators, many of whom have held principal positions, underestimate the challenges that building-level leaders face.

Central office leaders who held principal positions three to five years ago do not face the same challenges that today's do. Demographic shifts, free and reduced lunch dynamics, and regulatory changes all make today's principalships more stressful in many ways that they were in past years.

This is particularly true for central office staff who have never been principals or who were principals several years ago. The principalship looks very different today than it did ten to fifteen years ago with enhanced external accountability, more rigorous consequences for being identified on state improvement lists, greater legal expectations around topics such as bullying, special education, and related areas.

Moreover, central office administrators did not discuss their leadership teams in the same way that building-level leaders talked about their teacher teams. The latter group spoke at length about developing collaborative teams and fostering shared leadership opportunities. Furthermore, they discussed getting out of their offices and getting to know their staff and students on a personal level, especially if they were new to their role and to their current district.

District-level leaders did not talk about relationships in a similar way. None of those who were interviewed discussed getting out of their offices, getting into their buildings, and building relationships with their principals and assistant principals. This does not indicate that they devalue their building-level leaders but does provide insight into the lens through which they may view their daily tasks. While building-level leaders emphasized people throughout their interviews, district-level leaders commonly spoke issues surrounding time management and work-life balance.

Survey data also suggests differences in how building-level and district-level leaders approach topics such as on-the-job loneliness. Respondents were asked to cite their top three on-the-job stress relievers and then identify which of those was the most "high-leverage" for their success. In this case, a high-leverage item is one that if done well, positively impacts several aspects of job performance.

For building-level leaders, the most commonly identified high-leverage task was developing strong collaborative teams. Developing high-functioning teams relates directly to the stressors that building-level leaders identified in the survey data. When asked to identify their top three stressors at work, the most common responses involved conflicts with parents, mediating conflicts among staff members, and working with challenging students. People were at the center of all of their identified stressors.

Developing strong teams and identifying with students and staff was an oft-cited strategy for combating loneliness. Shaina, as a new high school principal, discussed leveraging her teams to build relationships and assist with delivering positive messages.

> I have learned to use the existing teams, such as the building planning team, to help brainstorm alternatives when a current plan is not working for people. Having a team that can help with those messages has been important.

Shaina has learned that to build trusting relationships, teams need to be empowered to be involved in the decision-making process. This collaborative process was cited again and again by building-level leaders as they discussed their job's core functions. Shaina's interview was consistent with survey data that indicated that principals and assistant principals view collaboration as a high-leverage strategy to combat their job's isolation.

Research on feelings of isolation and loneliness for leaders differentiates between those who transition from within the same organization and those who begin leadership careers in a new organization. For those who transition from teacher to leader within the same organization, feelings of isolation and loneliness may be significant. Nichols and McBride[1] studied four beginning educational leaders and their transitions from within the same organizations in which they taught. They found that their subject's technical skills were strong, but their relational skills varied to handle the abrupt shift.

Executive loneliness was marked by feelings of isolation from former peers and resentment emanating from some former colleagues. Colleagues who used to be friends suddenly treated their new supervisor differently. Most in their students noted that they were ill-prepared to handle the stark contrasts in relationships that occurred when moving from teacher to school leader.

Moreover, Nichols and McBride's study found that few educational leaders spoke of emotional supports during their transition.[2] Unlike teacher peer groups that can provide strong emotional support for life-changing events such as weddings, childbirth, loss of loved one, and other events, similar support did not appear to exist among leadership peer groups. Those relationships, according to their study, existed outside of the workplace among friends and family. This suggests that for school leaders building a strong peer network outside of the immediate workplace may be important.

Within the workplace, however, strategies outlined by those interviewed in this study reinforce what Nichols and McBride found. Building trusting relationships is a primary strategy toward breaking down feelings of isolation and loneliness. While not necessarily leading to friendships, it does build a caring and considerate school culture where all staff are valued and supported. School leaders must not become so attuned to the division of roles that they lose their ethic of caring of the staff they are leading. When promoted from within, this means navigating feelings of isolation and loneliness while simultaneously building trusting relationships with former colleagues.

Feelings of isolation and loneliness may be experienced differently by those promoted within the same organization as compared to those who change organizations. With the latter, peer groups do not carry over into the new leadership position. There may be more of a "clean break" when transitioning from teacher in one organization to administrator in a new organization. Starting as an administrator on day one in a new organization allows for school leaders to build new relationships around their formal leadership position rather than attempt to reconstruct those that were built in a collegial environment.

Moreover, some researchers have begun to challenge the oft-held notion that high-power positions lead to increased isolation and loneliness. While being the only principal in a building full of teachers, aides, support staff, and students can be professionally isolating and lonely, possessing power has also proven to make people more socially resilient.[3] Because power can enhance social opportunities, rewards specific social skills, and buffers against some social stressors, some researchers have suggested that those at the social hierarchy's bottom are actually lonelier than those at the top.

As an objective dynamic, school leaders often face isolation and loneliness. Within an organization, there are usually far more teachers and support staff by the numbers than there are administrators. Based purely on objective numbers, it would be easy to suggest that school leaders must be among the loneliest school staff. Subjectively, however, high-power positions may reduce the need to feel like one has to belong.

School leaders seek administrative positions with the full understanding that their words, actions, and deeds will stand out among their organizations. The formal authority and power possessed by school leaders necessitates this recognition and social distance from one's followers.

These power dynamics have important implications for strategies focused on reducing isolation and loneliness. Managers should be aware that those in less-powerful positions may feel isolated from decision-making and hungry for recognition. School leaders should consider ways to provide all employees with opportunities to attain power or at least feel powerful. This is often true especially for support staff such as paraprofessionals, custodial staff, and clerical employees. Although these staff truly keep an organization afloat, they are often overlooked when crafting committees or seeking input.

Attending to all employee's social needs, especially those with less formal power and job autonomy, is an important strategy for school leaders to pursue when combating isolation and loneliness. While this benefits the employee, it also benefits the school leader. Research has demonstrated that employees who feel valued are more likely to engage in organizational citizenship behaviors (OCBs). These actions, while not formally part of anyone's job, contribute to an organization's well-being.

OCBs include volunteering for after-school clubs or committees, attending parent-teacher organization meetings, and other nonpaid or extra-time activities that all organizations have. When school leaders bemoan the lack of participation among staff in these areas, the first thing to check is their employee's sense of belonging. Communicating their value to employees, especially support staff, often increases the likelihood that staff will engage in such behavior and go above and beyond to represent the school community.

Such recommendations circle all the way back to strategies geared toward building trusting relationships. When school staff feel valued by their administrator through a professional relationship, they are more likely to engage in collaboration with one another. Employees who feel valued are more likely to make difficult phone calls home, be proactive instead of reactive with students, and engage in the extra behaviors that often define a school's culture. Reducing leader isolation and loneliness involves reducing such feelings among school staff. When school staff feel valued and reciprocate those feelings toward their administrator, a truly collaborative culture can emerge.

School leaders can promote this culture by reflecting upon their daily interactions with students, staff, and families. Knowing student names, participating in and leading data meetings, and greeting families at the door at school concerns are only three strategies that will help any school leader build these relationships. Trust relies upon dependability. When a school community knows their leader is dependable and consistent, the beginnings of a trusting relationship are formed. Interviews, survey data, and research all indicate that focusing on these relationships is the more effective way to combat isolation and loneliness.

CHAPTER SUMMARY

In this chapter, prospective and practicing school leaders discussed isolation and loneliness as parts of their jobs. To combat these feelings, several strategies were discussed:

- Build trusting and authentic relationships with students, staff, and the community.
- Possess an ethic of care toward those being served.
- Recognize that power dynamics may be different when being promoted from within versus changing organizations for advancement.

NOTES

1. Joe Nichols and Jackie McBride, "Promoted from Within: Preparing Beginning Educational Leaders for Executive Loneliness that Occurs in their New Position," *College Student Journal*, 51, no. 1 (2017): 47–57.

2. Nichols and McBride, "Promoted from Within: Preparing Beginning Educational Leaders for Executive Loneliness that Occurs in their New Position," 50–52.

3. Adam Waits, Eileen Choi, Joe Magee and Adam Galinsky, "Not so Lonely at the Yop: The Relationship Between Power and Loneliness," *Organizational Behavior and Human Decision Process*, 130 (2015): 69–78.

Chapter 7

Preparing for the Shift and Navigating New Roles

EXPECT TO LEARN

In this chapter, prospective and practicing school leaders will learn that pursuing an administrative career requires deep reflection and thought. There are several reasons why teachers and other staff pursue administrative positions. These reasons also differed among survey respondents in interesting ways.

How do you know when you are ready to pursue an administrative career path? Most successful school leaders would have been practicing leadership long before entering an advanced studies program. Whether as a classroom teacher, athletic coach, extracurricular adviser, student teaching host, or other avenue, most practicing administrators began developing a leadership itch before starting their program. Entering administrative positions with the right mindset and for the right reasons are also important considerations for prospective school leaders.

Entering school leadership as a career to pursue professional challenge was a common theme throughout the interviews. Madison, a veteran school leader who is beginning her second full year as a large-school elementary principal, was forthright about her career path into administration. She has served in many leadership roles throughout her career including elementary literacy coach, secondary assistant principal and principal, and K-12 principal in a rural district. While appearing scattered, Madison could easily identify why her career path looks as it does.

> I want to end up in a central office position, perhaps as a Superintendent. I have gained a great perspective on K-12, rural to city, schools with systems and schools without systems. I wouldn't have gained all of that perspective had I

stayed in one system for my entire career. I think I have a clear picture at this point of what a successful district looks like.

Madison's overarching advice for prospective school leaders is to "know your why." It cannot be pleasing people, because that will never be possible in all cases. Moreover, Madison also outlined that someone's "why" should not be for money. In a common theme reiterated throughout the interviews, the money will never be enough to make up for the additional hours, the added stress, and the enhanced burden that school leaders carry.

As a brand-new principal with a young family and a thirty-minute commute one-way, Tony also emphasized the importance of entering administration for the right reasons. For him, he discussed his passion for helping teachers maximize their teaching ability. Moreover, Tony also emphasized that pursuing school leadership for the salary increase is a strategy that will backfire in the long run.

> The money is absolutely not worth doing it for. I think a lot of early career teachers see their veteran administrators and think they are rolling in the dough. Maybe they are because they have been earning that salary for several years and don't have young kids at home. I can tell you that I would guarantee I make less per hour now than I did as a teacher because I'm working so many more hours, which is not a complaint because I love what I'm doing.

Tony also touched on another topic that arose among many administrators: access to and use of power. Many teachers and other school staff pursue administration because they want to change their schools for the better. While appropriate, the approach that school leaders take in pursuing change can help or hinder their efforts. Ryan, a veteran school leader in his first year as an elementary principal, discussed how he has approached leading a new staff comprised of mostly veteran teachers.

> This is my 20th week now as principal. Zero directives. I have given zero. I've asked a ton of questions, I've made a lot of visits, but this building has a strong, solid veteran staff. It's different than leading a younger staff like I was used to. To be trusting, you have to trust.

Although armed with significant formal authority as building principal, Ryan realized that he needed to take time, listen, and observe before considering any structural changes. Symbolically, Ryan understands that by listening in a nonjudgmental manner, he will gain his veteran staff's trust quicker than if he employed a direct frontal assault on every problem. For many teachers, administrators come and go like the seasons. Prospective administrators should realize that staff members, particularly veteran staff members, want their principals to succeed but are also wary of a new principal instituting a new idea right from the start without getting to know the building's culture.

Several administrators spoke about preparedness for leadership positions as it relates to power. As discussed in the chapter on building relational trust, school leaders can only move their ideas forward by working alongside others. Whether it be staff, students, central office, fellow administrators, or the community, no one administrator is able to move a school forward in isolation. It takes long-term, intentional trust-building efforts. In many ways, school leaders are imbued with much formal authority but little actual direct power. Tony spoke about the counterintuitive nature of leadership and power.

> If you want power, you are going to find out that you have far less of it than you think you do. There are a whole lot of hurdles to imposing your will and you will find that it will end badly for you if you do. To be successful, you have to empower others around you. People have to walk with you.

Prospective school leaders should reflect upon their own attitude toward power and how they wield the power that they currently possess. As it turns out, adults often have far more complex lives than children do. School staffs are comprised of adults from all walks of life, socioeconomic income levels, racial and ethnic backgrounds, and diverse life experiences.

Whether they realize it or not, school leaders possess tremendous influence over how their staff experience their workdays and what attitudes they bring home to their own families. Whether staff leave work fulfilled with a good day's work or exhausted by another day in a chaotic system is often up to the school leader and their use of power.

Along with attitudes toward self-reflection, money, and power, school leaders talked about how prospective administrators could position themselves for future leadership roles. A common thread was advice around individual contributors to a system, such as teachers, gaining a broader perspective on how the system as a whole operates. Before earning her first formal administrative position as an assistant principal, Monica had gained valuable experience leading meetings in the special education world. In a part-time teaching, part-time leadership position, she gained valuable experience balancing various demands and personalities.

> I was a special education coordinator before landing this AP position. It really put me in a good position before being here. I was able to take on more responsibilities while teaching and that was good preparation. I can't imagine not having that experience under my belt.

Monica advised prospective administrators to find "pseudo-administrative" experiences within their current roles to take on additional learning and broaden their perspectives. While her role was formalized, several other experiences may be available to prospective administrators such as lead teacher positions, department chairs, and others. Gaining experience at having to say no to coworkers and having difficult conversations about teacher-related topics such as scheduling and room assignments can help prepare future school leaders for the challenges that lay ahead.

Greg's career path is a good example of seeking out such experiences. Although he only taught five years, he served on several building-level committees and chaired special education parent meetings. In addition, he was continuously seeking out principal as a mentor and finding ways to help with various initiatives. He led PTA projects, hosted building assemblies, and did whatever he could to make himself useful. He had similar advice for those seeking to pursue school leadership as a career.

> Take advantage of all of the little opportunities that exist within a school or district. I don't care how large or small your district is—they are out there if you look for them. Be on a scheduling team, the building planning team, take over one little initiative even if it's just something fun. Those things get your toes wet, and help you understand what it means when someone is irritated with you because you didn't handle things the exact same way they would have.

Experiencing the tension associated with having difficult conversations and telling people no was a common theme. So often, successful teachers thrive in the classroom because they are good at helping students and families. Moreover, there is a clear power distinction between students and teachers; the latter has access to formal power (i.e., grades) over a student's sense of progress and identity. Those power distinctions are less clear among adults.

Developing "thick skin" is necessary for all school leaders and can be difficult to learn when someone is used to being in a position of always being able to say yes. Part of school leadership is gatekeeping; we all work within a system and the system necessitates that some things are the way that they are. There are contractual limitations to reasons that employees can take benefit days, there are specific contractual working hours, and there are a multitude of rules and regulations that fall to the school leader to monitor compliance with.

Developing a thick skin entails engaging in uncomfortable conversations with employees when it would be easier just to let the behavior pass. Ryan spoke about his role with this dynamic.

You are the helper and the henchman. Tell me one principal that everybody loves. You can't. And you don't get to tell your side to the story as to why. Regardless of what the rumors are out there about you, there's always another side to the story, and you usually can't tell it.

Shaina entered her first year as a high school principal having been a secondary assistant principal for several years. She quickly learned that there are responsibilities that principals have that often aren't shared with their assistants. One of those is being the final authority in the building on many sticky situations. The principal is often the final rung on the decision-making ladder for many issues and it often falls to them to be the final word on whether an idea or issue is approved or not.

As a teacher, I was a people pleaser. In this role, you have to get used to people not liking you and that's okay. Did I do the best job that I did to support the students and staff in this building? It may have not made everyone happy, but that is something that people need to think about before they jump into any kind of school administrative role.

Richard had similar advice for prospective administrators. His career path includes middle school assistant principal, elementary principal, and now district-level special education director. Across all of those roles, he has learned that it is impossible to please everyone with any decision. His advice to prospective administrator was both straightforward and practical for consideration.

It's important to develop that thick skin and it's not realistic that you can please everyone. If you are pleasing everyone, something is probably wrong, to be honest. Accept that there will be letdowns. Understand that perception can be reality and don't take offense. Be clinical with decisions, not emotional.

Before stepping into a formal school leadership positions, prospective administrators can position themselves for success by seeking out opportunities to broaden their perspective and open up chances for difficult conversations. As uncomfortable as it can be to have to disagree with another adult, gaining experience with those conversations is crucial.

The survey data, moreover, demonstrated differences in reasons among men and women and building-level and district-level administrators for pursuing an administrative career path. Among administrators interviewed discernible differences did not come to the fore. The survey data, however, marks a clear difference in thinking among these groups.

In some areas, men and women differed little in their motivations for pursuing formal school leadership positions. Similar percentages of men (80%)

and women (81%) indicated that their desire to make a broader impact was among their main reasons for seeking administrative positions. Additionally, similar percentages of men (76%) and women (77%) marked their pursuit of greater professional challenge as a motivating factor. In terms of impact and professional challenge, little difference existed.

In two other areas, however, clear differences emerged from the data. First, exactly half (50%) of all male respondents indicated that increased pay was a prime reason for climbing the professional ladder within education.

Only 33% of female respondents, however, indicated that increased pay was primary. A desire to make more money typically runs counter to people's reasons for entering education; except at the very highest administrative levels, pay scales tend to be much less than what could be earned in the private sector. As we have seen, school leaders interviewed specifically warned prospective administrators from entering the field solely for the money. The increased hours and enhanced stress levels, for example, more than offset the salary increase.

Survey feedback is also insightful here. Administrators can respond with their true motivations more freely than they could in a face-to-face interview. It is possible, therefore, that increased pay is more of a motivating factor than those interviewed were comfortable discussing in person. Eschewing money to serve the greater good is an excellent public face to maintain when seeking positions that pay increasing higher salaries.

The second divergent data point among men and women involved power. Nearly 60% of male respondents noted that their increased ability to exert influence was a major motivation for pursuing administration compared to only 40% of females surveyed. Once again, this data differs from the trends revealed through interviews.

During the interviews, both male and female administrators cautioned prospective school leaders from seeking leadership positions to exercise power. They warned that, despite being in a formal position of authority, school leaders possess very little raw power. Rather, influence is earned by empowering and trusting others instead of overtly exercising authority.

Do men seek leadership positions for power more than women do? The survey would indicate that they do. Once again, when able to answer anonymously, survey respondents may be more likely to be truthful than during in-person interviews. Empowering others and facilitating leadership is the correct interview answer when asked about style; this survey data would indicate, however, that more school leaders perceive their increased power as another reason for taking on leadership positions.

Survey data differences also emerged among building-level and district-level administrative staff. Similarly, to the data comparison among men and women, approximately the same percentages (84% and 83%, respectively) of building-level and district-level school leaders cited their desire to broaden their impact as a main motivating factor for pursuing their position. In this instance, building-level administrators include both principals and assistant principals. In addition, nearly approximate percentages from both groups rated their ability to exert influence as a factor—50% and 43%, respectively.

Similar motivations end there, however. Interestingly, wide gaps were demonstrated among building-level (33%) and district-level administrators (60%) when considering increased pay. It may be true that many entry-level administrative positions, such as assistant principal, offer similar salaries to what a mid-career teacher would earn. Initially, earning more money may not be a primary consideration.

When district-level positions become available, however, they also often carry higher salaries. Large-school director positions and assistant superintendent positions are often responsible for large swaths of district functions and offer much higher salaries than building-level roles. Although district-level positions may not interact directly with students, school leaders may seek them out due to their higher salaries as they move further into their career paths.

Moreover, building-level and district-level administrators responded differently in terms of seeking professional challenge. While only 68% of building-level leaders cited greater professional challenge as a factor, nearly nine in ten (88%) of district-level administrators did so. Both groups demonstrated that this reason was crucial. District-level work, however, tends to be more complex in many ways than building-level work and this reason could account for the data difference.

At the district level, administrators are often handling issues that surround K-12 as a whole or multiple building concerns at once. Unlike building principals who can wrap their arms around their building and imprint their personality on its culture, district-level leaders often do not connect directly with staffs and school communities. The leadership challenge tends to be more multidimensional than at the building level.

The good news for prospective administrators is that 86% of those surveyed would "strongly encourage" or "encourage" teachers to pursue school leadership as a career path. Only 12% of respondents were "neutral" on the profession as a career choice and the very few remaining would not recommend administration as a path. Equally high numbers of building-level leaders (81%) and district-level leaders (88%) would either strongly encourage or encourage administrative careers.

Does administrative career satisfaction, however, wane as a school leader moves further into their career? The survey data indicates that possibility. Of untenured administrators, 90% would strongly encourage or encourage the career path compared to only 82% of those who have earned tenure. Both are very high, which is positive. While veteran administrators can move into positions where they are suddenly untenured, this data would indicate that brand-new school leaders may demonstrate more enthusiasm for their career choice than those with years under their belt.

Everyone enters their professional journey at a difference place and time. Family factors, financial dynamics, and professional readiness all play an important role. For those entering school leadership as an intentional career choice, these factors all intersect at some stage and trigger self-reflection. Each person's motivating factors will be both similar and different from everyone else's. The key for prospective school leaders is to understand their own professional journey, their own motivations, and their own reasons for undertaking these challenges. No one factor should push a great teacher into leaving the classroom to try to lead a building.

Vanessa's interview uncovered the best answer on advice for those considering either starting their certificate program or taking the leap into administration as a career. Her ten-year career in administration has traversed elementary school, middle school, and now district office. She has served as an assistant principal, principal, and district-level director all within the last four years after spending her first six years in the same position. She has recently changed districts, moreover, for the first time in her eighteen-year total career in education.

> You have to look at where your trajectory is. If you take a lead too early, you will miss out on growth that you need, but if you jump too late at a higher position, you may miss your boat. It's tricky. There are a lot of factors and none of them are wrong: what's your lifestyle? Can you take on more responsibility right now? How does that fit into your current life?

There is rarely a right answer when deciding when to jump in, but there may be a lot of wrong answers. Discussing with loved ones, reflecting on one's own professional and personal readiness, and seeking advice from strong mentors are all good steps. Sometimes the grass is greener on the other side, but often times it is not. Building-level and district-level positions are stressful. Classroom teaching and school administrative positions are both stressful, but often in different ways. And too often, those pursuing school leadership have not experienced the stress levels inherent in many leadership positions. Vanessa again had insightful advice on this topic.

> Regardless of your administrative position, 95% of the job will be great, and 5% will be difficult to navigate. That's just the way it seems to be. Be open to learning, as long as you know you're going to screw up and being okay with those things.

Being comfortable with oneself and one's own professional journey appear to be stabilizing factors, regardless of all of the other differences that were exposed in the interviews and survey data. Being "ready" is subjective, but self-reflection can help isolate the pros and cons that exist within any career move.

CHAPTER SUMMARY

When shifting into new leadership positions, it is important to reflect upon one's mission and values. The interviews and survey data both reflected that different leaders move into positions for different reasons. Most importantly, developing a thick skin and being comfortable with difficult conversations are important skill sets for school leaders.

Chapter 8

Survey Overview, Important Trends, and Takeaways

EXPECT TO LEARN

This chapter focuses on the survey tool that was used to gather school leader feedback on stress, balance, and strategies. In addition, the survey asked respondents several demographic questions. Filtering these questions uncovered interesting trends that school leaders may want to consider when navigating their career paths.

This study's main goal was to understand how practicing administrators experience their leadership positions on a day-to-day basis. Most importantly, it sought to uncover common themes across diverse leadership experiences from which prospective and practicing school leaders could learn. Moreover, it sought to provide professional development to prospective and practicing school leaders around topics such as time management and entry planning.

One method for understanding those experiences was face-to-face interviews. Thirteen school leaders were identified for interviews. Diverse administrators were sought for this study: from beginning to veteran school leaders, both men and women, those with older children and those with younger children, and those at the building level and those at the district level. These interviews uncovered several common themes on preparedness, thoughts on building relationships, feelings of isolation and loneliness, and advice on transitions that may be useful for prospective and practicing school leaders.

Survey data was another method utilized to gather day-to-day experiences among a broader group of school leaders. While the interviews yielded deeply personal transcripts, the survey data provided a broader picture of how many more school leaders feel about their jobs. This data helps reinforce themes uncovered during the interviews and provides further insight into how administrators handle stress, strategize for improvement, and perceive their leadership positions.

To gather this data, a Survey Monkey tool was designed and made available for school leaders over several social media platforms. Available in Appendix, the survey sought demographic information for participating school leaders and then asked them about their day-to-day stressors, how they overcome those stressors, and their feelings about their administrative positions.

Several interesting insights were uncovered throughout the survey that provide a snapshot of the profession at this moment in time. While many of those themes were discussed in previous chapters, this chapter seeks to provide a broader picture of respondents and their responses. Several categories provide deeper insight into who responded to the survey and how this shapes the survey data.

CAREER TRAJECTORY

First, approximately 50% of all survey respondents were within their first three years in their current positions. For many of them, this represents the first three years of their overall administrative career. The career-length range, for all respondents, was from one to nineteen years of administrative experience. It may be that pursuing a social media-driven strategy to publicize the survey resulted in a younger respondent pool. For whatever the reason, these survey results should be especially interesting to those just starting a new position or diving into their first administrative position on their career path.

CURRENT LEADERSHIP POSITION

Of survey respondents, district-level administrators represented the largest percentage of the total pool at 39%. While nearly one in four respondents' current administrative position was at the district-office level—either at the director or assistant superintendent level—only 9% of respondents' current work was at the middle school level. Additionally, school leaders at the elementary level accounted for approximately one-quarter (27%) of all respondents and those at the high school level accounted for one-quarter (25%) as well.

More middle school level respondents would have provided additional balance to the survey respondents. As a relatively new educational construct, "middle school" only emerged within the last thirty years as junior highs transitioned to include grade six in many districts. Middle school can be a unique leadership experience as students are only in such a setting for three years, compared to six years traditionally in elementary school and four years in high school.

Moreover, faculty and staff in middle school do not get to enjoy either the beginning of student's educational career in kindergarten or final destination with graduation. Additionally, middle school often encompasses the more challenging years for students as they grow up. Early adolescence is rarely any adult's most cherished memory. All of these factors make the middle school years a unique experience. More respondents from this level may have brought more balance to the survey.

GENDER AND MARITAL STATUS

Of survey respondents, 56% were female. That number was consistent among both building-level and district-level respondents. Interestingly, this was much higher than the national average where almost three-quarters of superintendents are male. Additionally, men are often overrepresented in positions that lead to the superintendency such as assistant superintendent and secondary principal roles. Education as a whole is predominately female, but leadership positions tend to be male-dominated. This survey ran counter to that trend and provided insight into how female school leaders feel about their profession. Many respondents were assistant principals, and it may be that females are equally represented in that job title. Superintendents were not considered for this survey as they were not the target group.

In addition, 87% of all survey respondents reported their status as married. Career moves into school leadership often occur mid-career; administrators in their early thirties are often considered young for their positions. With respondents overwhelmingly married, their responses to stressors may have been impacted. As with interview subjects, survey respondents stated that spending time with family was one of their high-leverage strategies for combating work-related stress. As marriage involves a give-and-take, as well, this may impact their approaches to building trusting relationships.

AGE AND ADMINISTRATIVE POSITION

In addition, respondents were asked to report their age range. Of respondents, 56% chose age ranges within the twenty-five to forty-four range, while 44% reported age ranges within forty-five to sixty-four. This wide range corresponds to the earlier discussion of time spent in current position. The range of responses included those in their first year as an administrator to school leaders approaching their twentieth year in the same position. Likewise, school leaders reported as large age range among survey respondents.

Diving deeper into response differences among ages twenty-five to forty-four and ages forty-five to sixty-four uncovered interesting comparisons.

Overall, the younger age range tended to be clustered at the building level, mostly untenured, more likely to seek school leadership to make a broader impact, and less likely to strongly encourage others to follow in their footsteps.

Among the younger age range, 69% held current building-level positions as principal or assistant principal while 31% worked in a district-level position. As administrative careers often begin at the building level, this trend may be expected. When asked to identify their main motivations for seeking school leadership positions, 85% selected a desire to broaden their impact among their responses.

While 55% of those ages twenty-five to forty-four reported high job satisfaction, only 36% reported that they would "strongly" encourage others to pursue school leadership as a career. This could reflect that newer school leaders, while highly enthusiastic, may take on too many responsibilities and be more prone to burnout early in their careers.

The older age range of forty-five to sixty-four was more likely to hold district-level positions than the younger age group. Of older respondents, 45% worked at a central office compared to only 31% of those in the twenty-five to forty-four age range. Moreover, those in the older age range were much more likely to be tenured; 56% reported their status at tenured compared to only 29% of those in the younger group.

Furthermore, older survey respondents were more likely to encourage others to follow in their footsteps. Of them, 57% reported high job satisfaction compared with 55% of those in the younger bracket. Additionally, 45% reported that they would "strongly" encourage others to pursue administration compared to only 36% in the younger range. While both groups reported similar job satisfaction, there was a clear difference in how strongly each group would encourage others to pursue school leadership.

HIGH-LEVERAGE STRESS RELIEVERS

Another area of difference was what strategies each group identified as their high-leverage stress relievers at work. In the survey, school leaders were asked to identify major stressors both at work and outside of work and then choose which of those they considered "high-leverage." In this context, a high-leverage strategy is one where if it was executed consistently, it would dramatically impact all other areas.

For the twenty-five to forty-four age group predominantly situated at the building level and untenured, the top identified high-leverage strategy involved building collaborative teams among staff. As we have seen, research has demonstrated that this strategy can combat feelings of isolation and loneliness. In both the interviews and the survey data, building strong teams around trusting relationships was cited over and over. Among the survey's younger demographic, this was the dominant theme. To no surprise, most school leaders in this group currently hold building-level positions.

For the ages forty-five to sixty-four demographic group, time-management effectiveness was identified as the top high-leverage strategy. This group was evenly split among the building-level and the district-level leaders. In addition, they were more likely to be tenured than the younger group. Their focus on managing time compared to building teams may reflect the group's stronger district-level presence. As the interviews demonstrated, school leaders at the district level were more likely to discuss their time management than their peers in principal or assistant principal positions.

Throughout the survey, several fault lines emerged with which to differentiate the data. Age, tenure status, leadership level, among others, provided filters for which to sort and sift the results for insights. Regardless of demographic area, the vast majority of school leaders noted that they would encourage others to pursue administration as a career. This fact reflects well upon the profession and should provide encouragement to those prospective administrators either pursuing their degrees or their first school leadership position.

CHAPTER SUMMARY

This chapter highlighted several ways in which survey data differed along demographic and career lines:

- Male versus female school leaders;
- Those newer to their current role and untenured versus those who have persisted in their current job for several years;
- Age ranges, particularly administrators ages twenty-five to forty-four and those ages forty-five to sixty-four, impacted how strongly school leaders would recommend others to follow in their footsteps.

In addition, strategies identified as "high leverage" for stress relief differed among building-level and district-level leaders. While the former emphasized relationship building, the latter group identified their own time-management practices as more important. "Where" an administrator is within their organization seems to have an impact on what factors they view as stressors and strategies to combat them.

Chapter 9

The Goose That Lays the Golden Egg
School Leadership and Time Management

EXPERT TO LEARN

Time management and stress around lack of time were common themes in our interviews and in the survey. In this chapter, concepts of time are reviewed and strategies discussed to enhance planning around time management. While leadership is unpredictable and the best-laid plans and go out the window by 8:00 a.m., planning for the week and day can have a positive impact on stress and leadership.

When identifying top stressors, 58% of survey respondents cited time management challenges as a concern. This perspective also emanated from several interviews. One new assistant principal, Rebecca, identified challenges managing more "open-ended" time than she experienced as a classroom teacher.

> When I was a classroom teacher, my time was really structured for me. We had bell schedules, blocks and periods, and contractual arrival and dismissal times. Now, as an administrator, those restrictions don't exist. Although it sounds odd to say, I struggle to manage my time when there aren't those boundaries. As an administrator, you don't have those constraints, but then you also have to choose more intentionally on what to spend your time on.

Approaching time as a resource that requires budgeting, like money, is a place to start. This resource-based time conception influences how and to what extent people manage their time. As a classroom teacher, with strict contractual boundaries, time within the workday is tightly managed. There are bell schedules, duty schedules, contractual arrival and dismissal times, prep time, lunchtime—the list goes on and on.

Transitioning from individual contributor to administrator, however, requires school leaders to reconceptualize the time management philosophy and practices. The manner in which leaders perceive their time awareness has significant implications for how they manage their time in an environment where there is always more to do.

Three concepts assist in identifying a school leader's relationship with time as a resource. First, school leaders should identify how they approach their time. Temporal awareness, as an idea, relates to "how much" control school leaders feel they have over their professional and personal time. Those with high temporal awareness prove adept at budgeting their time.

Conversely, those with low temporal awareness are always viewing time as "slipping away." These school leaders are always late for meetings, rarely complete tasks on time, and are always in need of reminders. A recommended strategy is reflecting upon one's relationship with time and feelings of control over time for not only new school leaders but practicing administrators as well.

Moreover, examining time structures can assist school leaders in achieving more self-efficacy in relationship to their time. Time structures are external aspects of one's time constraints that are visible. External factors such as deadlines, timing and duration of events, an organization's sense of urgency, among other dynamics, are time structure examples. These structures are explicit and formalized; grey areas do not exist.

For example, for building principals the weeks around state-mandated testing contain significant time structures. Typically, mandates exist that govern when tests are distributed, stored, and scored. During these weeks, time structures often dictate how school leaders budget their time. For example, during state testing weeks, building principals may be managing testing in their offices more than they are visible in cafeterias. Understanding these time structures and communicating them to staff can help school leaders and their communities more effectively manage time.

Other factors also influence time structures. A job's autonomy level often determines how much leeway school leaders have with their time. Often, a committee on special education chairperson who manages planned meetings all day will have more stringent time structures than a building principal, for example. Some school leadership jobs are more structured than others. When reflecting on professional fit, a positions built-in and nonnegotiable time structures are worth considering.

Time norms are the third concept for school leaders to consider. Time, as a concept, possess moral connotations. Organizations often have shared patterns of expected activity that influence how leaders spend their time. Every organization has a different culture around time. Time norms, unlike time structures, are often unwritten rules that are not perceptible to outsiders and sometimes taken for granted within organizations by those who work there.

One method to analyze an organization's time norms is to examine its relationship to email. While convenient for communicating quick points, email can become an overwhelming task for school leaders. Are there expectations about answering emails after work hours? When does the most senior leader send their emails? These questions can help uncover time norms as they often exist below the surface and can be difficult to fathom.

Greg, a veteran elementary building principal in a large district, described how he and his principal colleagues have banded together to reestablish time norms:

> Our principal group has decided that we are going to avoid emails after 4pm unless an emergency. If only one of us did that, and the other six kept right on, the one would stand out. We are trying to put out of office messages up to let people know that we are not going to be answering emails after a certain time.

Greg and his team's approach is important; when one person violates a time norm, it stands out. Often, those within the organization aren't aware that time norms even exist. A group approach is important here. When one person is able to leave work on time and appear unstressed yet others stay late, come in early, and appear stressed all the time, time norms may dictate how those approaches are perceived.

Most likely, the school leader who can manage their workload, leave on time, and manage their stress is far better at managing their time than others who pride themselves on "staying late." School leaders should consider an organization's time norms when scanning for jobs.

CREATING CONDITIONS FOR TIME MANAGEMENT

When school leaders accept administrative positions, they also accept new realities around time and expectations. It would be unrealistic to expect that school leaders can manage their time perfectly on any given day; they should reflect upon how they can create conditions to manage their time. Angry parents, staff conflicts, and endless emails will always exist; instead of trying to plan perfectly, school leaders can put systems into place that promote better planning.

Organizing time into quadrants is one method to reconceptualize our time. In his highly popular *The Seven Habits of Highly Effective People*, Stephen Covey discusses the Eisenhower Matrix as a time-management strategy.[1] This four-quadrant matrix, as illustrated in figure 9.1, categorizes time on two axes: Urgent-Not Urgent and Important-Not Important:

School leaders spend most of their official working hours in quadrant one. Interviewees and survey respondents consistently listed "angry

	Urgent	Not Urgent
Important	**Quadrant I** • Crisis • Pressing problems • Deadline driven projects	**Quadrant II** • Relationship building • Finding new opportunities • Long-term planning • Preventive activities • Personal growth • Recreation
Not Important	**Quadrant III** • Interruptions • Emails, calls, meetings • Popular activities • Proximate, pressing matters	**Quadrant IV** • Trivia, busy work • Time wasters • Some calls and emails • Pleasant activities

Figure 9.1 Urgent-Not Urgent and Important-Not Important.

parents," "staff issues," and other urgent and important tasks as the most time consuming and the most stressful. As aforementioned, time structures also come into play. As late August turns into early September, a host of tasks around opening school become pressing and thrust themselves to the forefront.

School leaders can, however, intentionally plan for quadrant two activities. Being intentional about relationship building, for example, is a high-leverage task that is both important and not urgent. There are always emails to answer, whereas lunch is served whether the principal is in the cafeteria or not. Being in the cafeteria and building relationships with students, staff, and families is higher-leverage than firing off dozens of emails, although it may not be urgent at that moment.

Differentiating quadrant three activities from those in quadrants one and two is important. School leaders can easily be sucked into non-important activities that steal large quantities of time. There is a difference between intentionally building relationships and engaging in meaningless, time-wasting conversations. Visiting classrooms on a daily basis to greet students is a quadrant two activity whereas spending thirty minutes talking about a football game while students are at recess is a time-waster. Being reflective and intentional about where tasks fall on the Eisenhower Matrix is the key.

While the Eisenhower Matrix provides a 30,000-foot view to analyze time, putting time management into practice requires a deeper dive. Once school leaders become more reflective about where their time goes, they may consider intentionally planning their week around their various tasks, meetings, and activities. A weekly planning grid is a tool that school leaders can utilize to preview their week, as illustrated in figure 9.2.

Week: _____	Three Main Goals: _____
Monday:	Tuesday:
5am	5am
6am	6am
7am	7am
8am	8am
9am	9am
10am	10am
11am	11am
12pm	12pm
1pm	1pm
2pm	2pm
3pm	3pm
4pm	4pm
5pm	5pm
6pm	6pm
7pm	7pm

Figure 9.2 Weekly Planning Grid.

This is a practical tool where school leaders, preferably on a Sunday evening before the hectic work week officially starts, lay out their calendars and intentionally plan their time. First, school leaders should put everything on the weekly grid that is on their calendar. This includes all meetings, events, and administrative tasks on their official calendars. Once quadrant one tasks are plotted, school leaders can then intentionally plot out quadrant two activities in the time that is remaining.

Most school leaders, when they first do this, are amazed at how much time is actually remaining. For example, very few school leaders are in meetings every day, all week. This may vary depending on different administrative roles, but building principals, for example, often have several short meetings throughout their week.

With the quadrant one (urgent and important) tasks laid out, school leaders can visualize their week and intentionally plan their quadrant two activities. Greeting students as they get off the bus, being present in the cafeteria and at recess, and other important but not urgent activities open up as possibilities when school leaders use such planning devices.

After weekly planning, the weekly grid can also be used as a personal accountability tool. Using the grid as a checklist throughout the week can help school leaders identify how they are spending their time. If a meeting is scheduled for one hour, for example, and it expands to two hours, the opportunity to be present in the cafeteria may be lost.

Reflecting upon "why" the meeting expanded is important. Was someone late? Was the agenda not followed and off-topic conversations allowed to dominate? Or, did the meeting end on time yet everyone continued engaging in friendly conversation well past its ending time? While friendly, collegial conversation itself can be positive, if every meeting expanded beyond its conclusion every time, quadrant two opportunities are lost.

When teams engage in this kind of planning, organizational change around time management is possible. Time norms can be uncovered by planning and then tracking time in this manner. For example, if meetings are always running long because some participants are allowed to continually ramble, a time norm has been discovered. It is incumbent upon school leaders to respect their own and their colleagues' time. Intentionally planning and then tracking time through a weekly grid can help school leaders become more reflective about their time management practices.

Taking the Eisenhower Matrix concept even deeper to weekly planning is important for creating the conditions to manage time well. Going from intentional weekly planning to intentional daily planning goes further. Utilizing a daily planning sheet, such as the example in figure 9.3, can help school leaders keep their quadrant one and two activities in focus.

A simple daily task sheet can help categorize urgent and important tasks as well as identify those tasks that are important but not urgent, such as writing thank-you cards. Clearly, an administrative will send more than handful of emails each day, but some of them will be more important than others and should be planned for.

| Daily Task Sheet | Date: _____ |

Phone Calls

Emails

Thank You's

Tasks

Meetings/Topics

Meeting	Time	Topics/Location

Hot List Going Forward

Figure 9.3 Daily Planning Sheet.

In addition, keeping a daily task sheet each day creates a historical work record that can be pulled from for important phone numbers and meeting dates. A recommended practice is to work on such a daily list two days at a time as conditions can change rapidly for school leaders on a daily basis.

Utilizing the Eisenhower Matrix, a weekly grid, and a daily task sheet are important for two reasons: First, they help school leaders be more reflective about their time management practices. Additionally, it helps create the conditions to manage time more effectively. A weekly grid completed on a Sunday evening may look very different come Friday morning depending on the week.

School leaders have unpredictable jobs and issues often arise without warning that demand immediate attention. Perfect planning is not attainable and is not a goal to pursue; rather, being more reflective about creating the conditions to manage time well is a goal worth pursuing for school leaders.

EMAIL: FRIEND OR ENEMY? OR FRENEMY?

Managing emails is consistently rated among school leaders' most time-consuming tasks. Most emails also fall into quadrant three on the Eisenhower Matrix. While most of them are urgent in the sender's eye, they may not be important. Utilizing the time-management concepts and tools discussed can help deliver sanity for school leaders around email practices.

First, school leaders should consider their time-management awareness specifically around email. As aforementioned, temporal awareness is the extent to which an individual believes they can control time as a limited resource. While our inboxes are like starfish—even when reduced, they always come back—school leaders can take steps to gain control over their email practices.

Moreover, school leaders should reflect upon their current email practices. How many emails does a school leader send and receive in a given day? What is the ratio of emails sent to emails received? How much time is spent reading, responding to, and sending emails? If our email program is constantly open on our computer screen, time can easily be lost endlessly replying to unimportant and not urgent emails.

Inherently, emailing is a quadrant three activity as it appears urgent but is usually not important. Some emails are important, of course, and the daily planning sheet discussed carves out space to intentionally plan for important emails. The average professional spends nearly one-third of their official work time responding to and sending emails. While some of that time is necessary, managing email clearly occupies too much time for most school leaders. Some of that time could be shifted to higher-leverage, quadrant two activities by reflecting upon email practices.

School leaders can take steps to bring their email time into proportion. First, school leaders should unsubscribe to every listserv to which they belong. Companies often send marketing emails to blanket groups. It is too easy to simply delete these emails; they will return the next day. Instead, school leaders should intentionally unsubscribe to everything. If a school leader receives five marketing emails a day, it will equal 35 such emails a week and over 120 such emails a month. Reducing an inbox by 120 emails on a monthly basis is progress. Sometimes, email software can automatically unsubscribe to such emails.

Additionally, school leaders should reflect on their philosophy around email replies. All school leaders want to be responsive to needs and be helpful. Taken too far, however, and work-life boundaries are jeopardized. Some emails do not need to be immediately answered; often, by taking a "wait-and-see" approach, insignificant problems will find their own solutions.

Do not avoid responding to crisis emails; if an angry parent emails, a quick reply email or (even better) a phone call demonstrates responsiveness and builds trust. Many staff and community members, however, send emotional emails rather than placing a phone call. Sometimes, letting an email sit for a few hours can strategically calm a situation.

In addition, school leaders demonstrate their availability over email and create expectations for rapid replies when they are not necessary. Quickly answering an email on a Friday evening while out to dinner with family or—even worse—quickly answering an unimportant email on vacation destroys any barrier created between home and work.

When responding *too* quickly to some emails, school leaders demonstrate that they can always be relied upon for a response. Therefore, the issue that can wait until Monday morning is more likely to intrude on a Friday evening date night. Letting an unimportant email sit over a weekend is strategically more important than responding immediately.

Finally, school leaders should reflect upon their communication practices as a whole. Email is sufficient for communication that calls for a one-dimensional approach; email lacks the ability to convey tone, body language, and other multidimensional communication techniques. Most communication, however, calls for face-to-face conversations or phone calls. This is especially true for emotional topics. Reflecting upon which type of communication medium is appropriate for different messages can also reduce a school leader's email load.

Often, a simple phone call can solve an issue that would have taken several email exchanges. Usually, face-to-face communication is more efficient and effective than one-dimensional email messages. Walking down the hall to deliver a message in person usually saves more time and sifting through numerous emails.

Time management is consistently ranked highly among school leadership's stressors. While school leaders can never fully plan for unpredictable days, they can create conditions that help utilize time more intentionally and effectively. School leaders should reflect upon their current time-management practices, undertake intentional weekly and daily planning, and reconceptualize their relationship with email.

Perfectly planned days do not exist in managerial work; with practice, however, school leaders can make it more likely that they are focusing on high-leverage activities rather than remaining bogged down in unimportant yet urgent tasks. As with leadership, in general, being reflective and intentional about one's practices are the keys to gaining more control over time.

CHAPTER SUMMARY

Reflecting upon time as a finite resource, similar to money, can help school leaders gain control over their time habits. Several strategies were shared in this chapter to help:

- Reflecting upon one's time concepts and awareness of where their time goes
- Employing visible strategies such as the Eisenhower Matrix, weekly planning sheets, and daily planning guides
- Taking a hard look at email practices. Reply practices, unsubscribing practices, and other strategies can help tame the email monster.

NOTE

1. S.R. Covey (2004). *The 7 habits of highly effective people: Restoring the character ethic.* New York: Free Press.

Chapter 10

Is It Time to Seek a New Opportunity?

Interviewing and Entry Planning

EXPECT TO LEARN

In this toolbox chapter, interviewing best practices are discussed along with successful entry planning. It is important to know when to pursue new positions and when to hold back. Reflecting current fit and work-life balance is crucial. In addition, having an entry plan during the interview process both organizes thoughts and assists the interview team in evaluating candidates. This can help put candidates ahead with interview teams when demonstrating that they have thought through their first few months in a new position.

Interviewing skills and entry planning are often not covered or taught in preservice programs. Matriculating through a program, earning certification, and completing an internship are key steps toward earning a first administrative position, but understanding how the hiring process works is also important. This chapter is designed to help newly certified administrators and those seeking new opportunities navigate best practices around applying for school leadership positions.

Throughout our interviews, practicing school administrators spoke about "professional fit" as instrumental to their success. Opportunities are not created equal; preservice and practicing school leaders should consider a host of factors when deciding whether to pursue different positions. There are several factors a school leader should consider when deciding whether to pursue specific leadership positions.

FAMILY PHASE

Educators pursue school leadership because they want to make a difference in the broader community. While noble, this goal should not come at the expense of the most important people in our lives: our family. Considering where one is in their family life is crucial. For example, taking on a building principalship and being the face of the building while having young children can be challenging. Several evening and weekend expectations could exist that may conflict with family priorities.

Balancing work and life in such a manner is not impossible, but it does require honest conversations about time commitments with family. Trading off possible career advancement to prioritize family may be the right decision for different phases in a school leader's life.

PROFESSIONAL FIT

Fitting into a position at stages in a career is often more important than rapid advancement. When a school leader experiences "professional fit," several factors align that contribute to career fulfillment: a positive leadership culture, supportive superiors, job stability, and work-life balance. While enticing to climb the career ladder rapidly, school leaders should consider a long-term career plan and where their current positions fit into that plan.

Being in the right place, at the right time, in one's career is more important than the accolades that come with rapid advancement. Climbing the ladder too rapidly and without reflection may lead to career misalignment, which can be more damaging than remaining in a current position for an additional year or two.

SUCCESS'S PERILS

Enjoying early career success may lead to enhanced opportunities within a short period of time. Connected with professional fit, guarding against being pushed or pulled into a promotion too early is a consideration. In many instances, demonstrating success in one position leads to opportunities to pursue "higher" positions. Success as an assistant principal, for example, may open principal opportunities quickly. School leaders should reflect deeply about their own career path and their desired end point. While praise feels good and accolades are hard to resist, school leaders should consider their own priorities before succumbing to an opportunity simply because it is offered.

Other factors exist beyond the three listed above. Ultimately, school leaders should be reflective about which opportunities they wish to pursue in light of their family life, lifestyle, career path, and other dynamics. Remaining in a great fit for a few more years is far better than jumping to a promotion that leads to work-life imbalance. Usually, great opportunities will exist for successful school leaders one, three, and five years in the future.

Once deciding to apply, a proper scan and entry plan are important. Depending on the actual position applied for, several avenues exist for research and analysis. To provide an example, this chapter will assume that a school leader is applying for an elementary-level principal position. Given that, there are several factors to consider when scanning a position for background information.

PREVIOUS PRINCIPAL TENURE

Has the building experienced turnover in principal leadership over the last few years? Or, has there been one building principal in place for over a decade? Answers to these questions often dictate what interview committees are looking for in principal candidates. If the building has experienced significant turnover, a committee may want to know a candidate's long-term career plans. For candidates who wish to end their careers as superintendents, such a building may not be the best fit if it is to serve as a stepping-stone to a district-level position. Conversely, if a building has had the same principal for over a decade, a shorter leadership tenure may be more palatable.

EXPECTATIONS VERSUS LIFESTYLE

As mentioned above, family phase plays a major role in determining professional fit. Many elementary schools have active parent organizations and community connections. As principal (as opposed to an assistant principal, for example), expectations can exist for being visible at all major events. Parents of younger students, in particular, want to know their child's principal and build a relationship with them.

Positives and negatives exist toward working and living in the same community, but integrating work and life into similar events can help school leaders navigate this factor. For example, if the elementary school is close to where the principal lives, they may be able to drive home for a quick family dinner before going back to work for a parent meeting. School leaders should pursue positions where they give themselves to their school communities in a reasonable manner without sacrificing their families.

WHAT IS THE SCHOOL COMMUNITY LOOKING FOR?

This is often the most important question to ask and should be intentionally pursued long before an interview is scheduled. School leaders should consider the answers to this question in light of their own skill set. For example, if school staff are looking for a principal to handle disciplinary issues but a candidate's strengths are around curriculum and instruction, the fit may not be ideal. In other cases, a school may be identified on a state improvement list and is seeking a curricular leader to form professional learning communities. School leaders should consider their own skill sets and knowledge bases when answering this important question.

Scanning an administrative position for potential fit can take many forms. A school's website is often a good starting point. Attention paid to a website—or lack thereof—by a school leader can inform many questions. Often, school websites contain information on programs, teacher classroom pages, photo galleries, and other aspects that can help candidates learn about the school community. In addition, larger district websites can inform questions about school budgets, administrative structure, and Board of Education topics, as well.

Social media platforms are also informative. Most school districts have Twitter profiles and, in many cases, individual employees also have their own Twitter handles. While Twitter tends to highlight a school's positive aspects more than its challenges, candidates can glean information on programs through such platforms. Often, checking into Twitter followers or other social media platforms can lead to mutual connections that can yield valuable information for scanning a principal position.

Moreover, state accountability report cards are excellent data sources for school buildings and districts. Candidates should never go into an interview without being intimately familiar with a school's accountability data. The data need not be memorized, but having a few talking points ready is warranted. Where do gaps exist? In what areas has a school performed well? Demonstrating to an interview committee that the candidate has done their homework and knows their school data is a must.

Finally, the least technologically advanced informational gathering methods are often the best: in-person conversations. Within most regions, teachers and staff have connections within different districts. Candidates can seek out actual employees within the school to which they are applying to ask the following questions:

- What are you most proud of about your school?
- What is the biggest challenge?
- What do you think the school community is looking for in a principal?

Candidates should never go into an interview without doing extensive homework on an opening. Demonstrating to an interview committee that the candidate has a working knowledge of the school community, its history, its data, and its challenges is essential. Candidates need not be experts on a school, but doing homework and conveying working knowledge in an interview demonstrates that they care enough to spend time on research before the interview takes place.

THE ENTRY PLAN—PUTTING RESEARCH INTO ACTION

All school leadership positions are important enough for candidates to spend time on an entry plan. The final product is not the only benefit; thinking through a school community and its leadership potential helps candidates organize their thoughts for interview answers as well. The process is as important, if not more so, than the final product.

The entry plans should begin considering the transition before the new position's first day. Using our earlier elementary principal example, the entry plan should begin with the time period before day one, if that opportunity exists. Many transitions involve the summer season as a time before student return in the fall. If possible, this is an opportune time for a new school leader to get to know their community before students return in earnest.

Welcoming parents and teachers to meet individually or in small groups during the summer months can build relationships that the school year's rush cannot allow for. Once students return, principals will not possess the bandwidth to put in this type of mass listening on a daily basis. A strong entry plan is built around listening to important groups and key contributors to a school's success. Intentionally planning for these meetings is the mental groundwork that leads to a solid entry plan.

A good entry plan considers three phases for transition: "pre-learning" to take place before a new position begins, considerations for the first three months on the job, and focus areas for the first six months. Intentionally planning for and being accountable to a six-month entry plan serves two purposes. First, it focuses a new principal on the Quadrant II activities necessary to build positive, trusting relationships. Moreover, it facilitates thoughtful interview responses and informed questions for candidates when they are sitting in front of a committee for consideration. As mentioned, the process and the product are both important.

An "inside-out" approach to planning for these meetings is recommended. Building principals, for example, will have the most frequent interactions with those within their main office areas on and their leadership teams. Scheduling time with building secretaries, other clerical staff, the school nurse, the head custodian, and any assistant principals is a recommended first step.

Often these key contributors will "carry the water" for a building principal when they cannot be available for every interaction. How positive is the building secretary's tone when they greet visitors? How clean is the building on a daily basis? When a student goes to the nurse, how is that communicated home? These key team members represent the building principal in their interactions with the larger community. They are crucial to establishing a building's culture; the culture, in turn, takes its cues from the principal. Scheduling time with and listening deeply to these key contributors should be a priority for any entry plan.

Meeting with teaching and support staff is the next ring on the "inside-out" approach to entry planning. Asking a few, culture-laden questions and listening intently to their responses is important. Asking staff about what makes them proud will reveal trends that help identify a school's strong points.

Moreover, asking staff about needed improvements will uncover areas that may require immediate attention, especially if they entail student and staff safety. Ask permission to take brief notes during these meetings and review these notes after several meetings to help discern these trends.

As a new school leader, it is important to realize while *you* are new to the school, many staff members may have worked there for several years. Therefore, it is important to honor the existing culture. New leaders should consider, if their position allows for it, a brief culture survey where staff can respond anonymously to questions. It can be powerful to ask staff to share thoughts on what makes them proud and what needs improvement. It helps to reinforce strengths among staff and identify common areas of concern. It also gives a new building principal a powerful point of departure for change, if necessary.

Finally, consider engaging with the broader school community. Early meetings with parent association leadership can lead to broader welcome-back events such as ice cream socials and playground night outs. Chances are that at least one parent association member was on the initial interview committee; leveraging this relationship to learn about the broader community may yield results. Credibility with parents and guardians can accelerate the process of gaining credibility with staff, and vice versa. The more positive conversations that take place about the school community the better.

While relationships are the entry plan's bedrock, there are other practical considerations to build into a six-month entry plan. Principals are similar to small-town mayors in that they are responsible for every facet of the building, even if they are not directly responsible for it. Therefore, having working knowledge of the physical plant is important. Building a trusting relationship with the head custodian is crucial. Spending time walking through the building, through each room, and the outside perimeter with the head custodian and custodial team is recommended.

While time exists for learning in many areas, student safety should be a priority for an entry plan's focus. Understanding school policies on community visitors, building entry points, and student medications is important. One major focus area should be the Building Safety Team. Convening a safety team meeting to listen to and learn from its members on their concerns should be an early step. In addition, while not necessarily an action step, engaging in daily building walk-throughs before students and staff arrive help familiarize a building principal with their physical plant and also identify areas for safety enhancements.

To illustrate these ideas further, a sample entry plan may be found at the end of this chapter (table 10.1). The plan contains three overarching entry plan goals to focus a new school leader's effort. These goals should also be high-leverage; doing them well will lead to success in many other areas. In addition, each entry plan action is aligned to professional learning standards. Finally, it is important to be accountable for the entry plan's progress. Checking off and initialing when these steps are complete will provide a self-check for new school leaders to measure their transition progress.

The entry plan sample may be adapted to several formats or templates. As long as it is focused on building high-leverage relationships, action steps may look similar or different. Thinking through a plan before the interview process, and then sharing with the interview committee, helps to organize a candidate's thoughts for a possible transition to a new position.

CHAPTER SUMMARY

Knowing when the time is right for a new venture is crucial for school leaders. Assessing professional fit, lifestyle, and other factors is important before jumping to a new position. When interviewing for new positions, school leaders should consider the following:

- Do homework on the new organization and prepare a handful of talking points.
- Prepare an entry plan to refer to and share with the interview committee.
- Be authentic and know who you are: the worst possible outcome is to fail to be transparent with an interview committee and end up in a poor professional fit, regardless of pay or prestige.

Table 10.1 Strands to Achieve Overarching Goals—Connections to 2017 Professional Standards for Educational Leaders (Formerly Known as ISLLC)

Actions	Standards Met	Completion Date(s)	Completion Check/Initial
A. Community/Collaborative Strand			
1. Create/send letter of introduction to parents/guardians of incoming K-5 students	2.A 4.C 4.D 6.A	July–August	
2. Reach out to all staff, in writing, via phone, over email, to informally meet over the summer—informally discuss school's strengths, areas of improvement, etc.	2.A 3.D 5.B	July–August	
3. Reach out to community businesses and elicit support for ongoing school activities	1.A 4.B 4.D	July–August	
4. Contact building planning team and board of education liaison to review previous goals and discuss vision for upcoming year	1.A 1.C 1.D 6.C	July–September	
B. Instructional Leadership Strand			
1. Become familiar with master schedule, teacher-student loads, and instructional programs—ensure that current programs are consistent with state mandates and research-based best practice	2.B 2.G 3.B 3.E 5.E	July–October	
2. Review and analyze student assessment data, including, but not limited to, the following: - state assessments, local assessments, benchmark data - disaggregate by subgroups	1.B 2.E 4.A 5.A 5.C 6.C	July–September	

3. Evaluate response to intervention process/progress in relation to research-based best practice and state mandates	1.B 1.E 2.E 2.F 2.G	August–October
4. Interface with district and building-level leaders to understand and successfully implement new initiatives and programs	1.A 2.B 6.C	August–December
C. Physical Plant/Safety Strand		
1. Conduct building safety inspection with head custodian and director of facilities and grounds—familiarize self with exit locations, "blind spots," and potential concerns	3.A 3.C 6.A	July–August
2. Review safety procedure drills (fire, bomb, intruder, severe weather, etc.)	3.C 5.D 6.A	July–August
3. Meet with safety team to review procedures, policies, and practices	3.C 3.D 1.A	September–October
D. Instructional Management Strand		
1. Review board of education policies in relation to building-level practices to ensure consistency	3.A 3.B	July–August
2. Review employee contracts (teachers, support staff, etc.)	3.A 5.D	July–August
3. Review budgetary lines, petty cash procedures, and other financial applications at building level	3.A 3.B	July–August

SAMPLE ENTRY PLAN—ELEMENTARY PRINCIPAL POSITION

Overarching Entry Plan Goals:

1. To establish professional, constructive, and positive relationships with students, staff, and stakeholder groups.
2. To further understand the school's professional learning community, physical plant, and financial/personnel practices.
3. To engage the school community in advancing a shared vision of school success that promotes the academic, emotional, and social well-being of all students and staff.

Chapter 11

Must-Read Books for Prospective and Practicing School Leaders

EXPECT TO LEARN

In this toolbox chapter, school leaders will preview several important books for their practice. While some are practical in nature, others are theoretical. A mix of both approaches will help equip school leaders with skills needed to succeed in a stressful and conflict-ridden leadership environment.

Lencioni, Patrick. 2000. *The Four Obsessions of an Extraordinary Executive.* **San Francisco: Jossey-Bass.**

Patrick Lencioni's books should be must-reads for any practicing or emerging school leader. Along with *The Four Obsessions of an Extraordinary Executive*, Lencioni has written several other leadership tracts. He writes in story form; rather than a research-based approach, Lencioni's books read as leadership fables and can be consumed easily in a handful of evenings or sittings.

The story's protagonist, Rich, is a visionary leader who builds his consulting company around a mysterious four-tenet sheet taped to his desk. Once an eighty-hour-per-week CEO struggling to maintain family life, Rich undergoes an epiphany and centers his leadership around one simple question: "What is the one thing I do that really matters to the firm" (p.16)? Upon reflection, Rich focuses on four disciplines and delegates strategy, implementation, and execution to his team.

First, Rich focuses on building a cohesive leadership team. He is personally involved with all leadership hiring and spends several hours with new management hires to orient them to the firm's culture. He ensures that all leadership team members buy in the organization's mission and values. Second, he continually reinforces organizational clarity (Discipline Two) by constantly overcommunicating mission and vision (Discipline Three). Finally, he promotes this clarity by personally investing in human systems. Managing performance, rewards and recognitions, and employee dismissal procedures have more to do with the "professional fit" than they do with results. Rich realizes that if his organization is healthy and cohesive, results will take care of themselves.

Lencioni tells this story by outlining one of Rich's few hiring mistakes. When a senior leader who does not share these values slips into the management team, organizational health is compromised. As Lencioni tells the story, it becomes clear that only one bad hire can poison an entire team. By failing to personally invest in this one bad hire, Rich compromises—for a time—the strict organizational discipline that he worked so hard to build.

School leaders will find several relevant lessons. First, as human resource–intensive organizations, the most important task schools undertake is employee hiring, onboarding, and management. As Lencioni writes, "Healthy organizations look for qualities in job candidates that match the values of the company" (p. 175).

School leaders, especially those who act as gatekeepers for hiring and firing, would especially benefit from Lencioni's work. When hiring candidates, we often overvalue certain items to the detriment of others. For schools valuing candidates with an equity mindset, for example, rich student teaching experiences in diverse settings may be more important than a high GPA or a stellar reference from their professor. Schools should get clear about what they value and then hire based on those values.

Moreover, Rich's central question to himself is the same question school leaders should be asking themselves: What are the high-leverage activities that school leaders should personally undertake to drive student outcomes? For building principals, for example, those activities are most likely ones that revolve around people such as building relationships with stakeholders, onboarding new employees, and related work.

After nearly burning out and selling his company by trying to do everything, Rich realized that he could only survive by focusing on those activities. Interestingly, this is also when Rich's firm's outcomes skyrocketed. By focusing on central tenets and empowering others to focus on their specialty areas, Rich built his leadership team as a team of experts rather than those always looking to the leader for direction.

Although not the book's focus, the reader is also struck by Rich's humility. His office is not flashy. He does not concern himself with his competition's latest initiatives. Rather, he remains focused on his four disciplines and empowers those around him to focus on the rest.

School leaders would be wise to emulate this approach to identify core values, reinforce those values through hiring and employee management, and empower others to focus on execution. While school leaders should not be hands off completely, many problems can best be solved by those closest to the problem. School leaders will find value in Lencioni's work and be surprised at how quickly this book can be read from start to finish.

Evans, Robert. 1996. *The Human Side of School Change.* **San Francisco: Jossey-Bass.**

Most teachers and service providers pursue school leadership because they want to serve others and improve student's lives. Often, that includes challenging the status quo. Moreover, change has been constant throughout education over the last several decades. This desire for improvement and continuous shifts in policy from the state and federal levels have resulted in constant change initiatives for school leaders to consider.

Evans's work highlights how this constant change uniquely impacts school systems and those who work in them. It also reinforces the value of building intentional relationships and investing first in human capital before initiating any change efforts. As Evans writes, there is a need for "a sympathetic principal who will acknowledge the distress they (teachers) are experiencing even as she reconfirms the promise of change and reinforces the necessity and promise of the new skills required" (p. 62).

Understanding that schools are unique as professional career paths is essential. Evans discusses the traditional career trajectory for professional school staff and how it impacts continuous change efforts. New hires in their twenties who stay late, continually attend professional development, read articles, and willingly make home visits often transition to mid-career professionals who are reluctant to continue those endeavors.

As Evans writes, "The first is a shift from the primacy of the work role in people's lives towards a primary of their personal roles" (p. 103). As professionals grow into their thirties and forties and reach mid-career, they often have spouses and children, homes with hot water heaters that fail on winter's coldest night, and health issues that did not exist immediately after college.

In addition, traditionally teachers have remained in one or two jobs their entire career. Although current generations may shift this paradigm, traditionally teachers persist longer in their assignments than other professionals. Evans writes that "fully three-quarters of all teachers have been teaching for at least fifteen years, and one-quarter for at least twenty years" (p. 94). This career stability breeds attachment to the status quo, especially as personal lives grow in importance over professional lives as staff grow older and take on additional adult responsibilities.

Evans's chapter on understanding reluctant faculty should be a must-read for all aspiring school leaders. Despite three decades of test-driven and data-centric reform efforts, most school metrics remain flat. Learning gaps among subgroups remain large despite new mandates, increased funding, and rigorous accountability measures. Why? As Evans notes, "Since standard measures used to motivate change don't work, we need to find others that do" (p. 115).

To accomplish this, Evans urges school leaders to look beyond technical components of change and focus on people. Building trusting relationships must come before school leaders ask staff to reconsider the practices they have employed for most of their careers.

Similar to Lencioni's story about Rich, Evans lands on clarity as the key to people-centered change efforts. Evans calls for an end to "the notion that we can motivate exceptional effort and performance merely by cramming a bloated improvement agenda through a faddish planning process" (p. 212). It begins with high trust levels. When school leaders build trust through interpersonal relationships, the workplace becomes more compatible with change efforts as staff are more likely to cooperate and better able to tolerate stress. With trusting relationships in place, school leaders are positioned to deliver change messages that focus on clarity and coherence rather than technocratic lingo.

To provide clarity, school leaders "target their energies, centering their time and effort on a short list of key issues, even if this means ignoring others" (p. 217). School leaders must make decisions around comparative importance. Leading this decision-making process also means deciding what to stop spending time on. Providing clarity on what is important also means providing clarity on what is not important—at least not immediately. For example, curriculum changes trickle down from state and federal policymakers at rapid rates; which changes should be considered first? Choices need to be made and communicated to staff to help them understand where priorities lay.

Evans calls for a different kind of leadership than is often promoted in school reform movements and preservice courses. It revolves around recognition rather than clinical observation or test-score graphs. He writes, "The single best low-cost, high-leverage way to improvement performance, morale, and the climate for change is to dramatically increase the levels of meaningful recognition for—and among—educators" (p. 254). Supply and demand levels rise and fall as change increases. When demand for changes rises, support for people must rise proportionally or else stress will. This calls for a different kind of leadership: away from the technocratic data analyst and toward an artful relationship builder.

While schools focus on student self-esteem, they often fail to concurrently do so for their staff. Recognition's most valuable face is a school leader who will listen to staff and one who can confirm that they have heard the extent and intensity of people's concerns. This extends beyond challenges within the school doors. Knowing staff personally, understanding their personal challenges, and recognizing that you have immense power over their lives are keys.

As supervisors, school leaders possess the ability to influence how staff feel when they arrive at school to start the day and leave to return home. Investing in these basic relationships is the first necessary step toward any school improvement effort.

Heifetz, Ronald and Linsky, Marty. 2002. *Leadership on the Line: Staying Alive through the Dangers of Leading.* **Boston: Harvard Business School Publishing.**

Leadership on the Line is a must-read for practicing and aspiring school leaders. Heifetz and Linsky take a technical approach to people-centered leadership through stories, anecdotes, and research. Importantly, they distinguish between technical changes and adaptive changes faced by organizations. For the former, current know-how and top-down leadership styles typically suffice. In schools, this concept applies to traditional master scheduling, assigning detention as a punishment for misbehavior, and similar concepts. Typically, school leaders possess the legal and technical competence to carry out these tasks.

Adaptive changes, however, require a different skill set and resonate with the themes outlined in earlier chapters. With adaptive changes (or what Robert Marzano would call "Type II Problems"), new problems require new approaches. This type of change requires that those closest to the problem engage in the solution. These changes usually challenge the status quo and require a different leadership approach than the traditional technocratic outlook. Most importantly, those experiencing these changes at the ground level should be involved in finding their solutions. It is less top-down and more democratic in approach.

Juxtaposing technical and adaptive challenges frame Heifetz and Linksy's study. Similar to Evans, they focus on the people-centered challenges around leadership. Especially when pursuing adaptive change, leaders will be asking staff to shed their status quo and take on new learning. This disequilibrium causes staff to react in different ways. Leaders would be wise to reframe resistance as part of the process. Recognizing the human side of change, Heifetz and Linsky encourage leaders to realize that strong reactions indicate that adaptive change resonates with followers. As the authors state, "In times of adaptive stress, groups exert pressure on people in authority to solve the problems that seem to be causing it" (p. 71).

Adaptive change, however, requires a decentralized approach even as leadership stress reinforces a traditional approach. To the authors, this is why most leaders fail. They encourage leaders to "Get on the Balcony" and take a holistic view of the players, the pressures, and the problems. To do so requires leaders to differentiate between themselves and their roles.

Heifetz and Linsky's most powerful chapters may be chapters nine and ten where they discuss how leadership stress can break down self-concept between role and self. In times of success and failure, leaders may be tempted to identify with their roles and personalize either praise or criticism. Encouraging leaders to reframe both in a depersonalized sense, they write, "Confusing role with self is a trap. Even though you may put all of yourself into your role—your passion, values, and artistry—the people in your setting will be reaching to you, not primarily as a person, but as the role you take in their lives" (p. 188).

While school leaders should build personal relationships with their staff, their relationship will be centered around work roles, not personal lives. The authors urge their readers to keep both allies and confidants but not confuse the roles, to seek sanctuary in turbulent times, and to remain anchored on self. Only in this way will school leaders maintain the distance between work role and self; with that understanding, it becomes possible to undertake significant work stress and still maintain self-confidence, poise, and balance.

Carnegie, Dale. 1936. *How to Win Friends and Influence People.* **New York: Simon & Schuster, Inc.**

Dale Carnegie's all-time classic should be mandatory reading for any professional whose job includes interfacing with people in a face-to-face environment. The first chapter—"If You Want to Gather Honey, Don't Kick Over the Beehive"—sets the tone for the rest of the book. Written in practical language and centered on relatable stories, Carnegie's core tenets include never criticizing, condemning, or complaining; becoming a good listener; and always attenuating the positive in personal relationships.

Two chapters are worth of note. First, Chapter One in Part Two is entitled "Do This and You'll Be Welcome Anywhere." In this chapter, Carnegie challenges his readers to rid their vocabulary of "I" and speak in terms of other people's interests. In carrying out this philosophy, school leaders need to build intentional relationships with their staff. As we have seen, this not only connects to Evans's work in *The Human Side of School Change* but also reinforces several themes throughout the book. Carnegie writes, "If we want to make friends, let's put ourselves out to do things for other people—things that require time, energy, unselfishness, and thoughtfulness" (p.60).

While school leadership is not about making friends, Carnegie's point concerning service to others is well-taken. As we have seen, school leaders who seek to serve their community and not themselves not only are less stressed but have a greater impact on their students and staff. Leading with service also requires working hard to see situations from someone else's point of view. On page 175, Carnegie writes, "Tomorrow, before asking anyone to put out a fire or buy your product or contribute to your favorite charity, why not pause and close your eyes and try to think of the whole thing from another person's point of view?"

Whether an angry parent, reluctant staff member, or challenging superintendent, reframing problems from another's point of view is useful. Often, the angry parent is simply advocating for their child in the only way they know how. It may not be your way, but it is the best they can do in the moment. Seeing this situation from the angry parent's point of view—perhaps they themselves had a negative school experience and do not trust the school system—can defuse tension. Finding common ground necessitates attempting to perceive such situations from another's point of view.

This perspective also validates their feelings. As Carnegie writes, "You will find examples of the futility of criticism bristling on a thousand pages of history" (p. 6). Criticizing rather than attempting to understand only backs other people into a corner. Once in a corner, they can only fight their way out. Rather than back the angry parent or reluctant staff member into a corner, reframing the situation from their point makes it much more likely that common ground can be found.

Carnegie's classic 1936 work is still relevant, if not more so, in today's fast-paced leadership environment. Slowing down, building relationships, and understanding our constituents are all strategies that Carnegie would embrace today.

Marotta, Andrew. 2017. *The Principal: Surviving & Thriving*. New York: Andrew Marotta, LLC.

Andrew Marotta, a principal in Port Jervis, New York, self-published this practical leadership guide for those in building leadership positions. Organized into 125 pragmatic tips and stories, Marotta's 140-page book is ideal for practicing and aspiring building-level leaders who focus on day-to-day leadership tasks.

His first chapter sets the tone for the book. Entitled "Be a Better Leader," this chapter's fourth tip is to "Don't be, look, or act defeated" (p.6). Marotta correctly indicates that school leaders' emotional states are contagious for their staff. He writes that "even if you inevitably feel in over your head sometimes, do not let it show. Snap out of it and look the part (p.6)." Especially at the building level, school leaders have hundreds of little interactions every day. In this fast-paced environment, there is time for some in-depth conversations, but most interactions take place in the hallway, the lunchroom, or during classroom visits. Hundreds of quick, positive interactions can accumulate into a positive building culture.

Many of Marotta's tips revolve around building trust with students, staff, and the community. Tip 63 is "don't hush-hush complicated episodes" (p.69). Ignoring problems and concerns break down trust between school leaders and their constituencies. When school leaders are humble enough to realize they need to seek guidance and vulnerable enough to ask for help, trust is built with stakeholder groups. When trusting relationships are in place, school communities are more willing to assist a school leader in solving a problematic issue rather than assigning blame for its existence.

Moreover, Marotta delves into several leadership topics on stress and well-being. Tip 117—"It's not personal" (p. 131).—is important as school leaders often have to deliver bad news to those that they serve. Similar to Heifetz and Linsky's discussion of role and self-separation, Marotta encourages school leaders to remember that their professional roles often necessitate difficult conversations. This does not make them easier; rather, it reframes them into a professional sphere where reactions can be expected. No staff member likes hearing that their lesson did not meet standards. Individual teachers, however, are not responsible for maintaining teaching standards across the entire building. School leaders hold this responsibility and have to do what is best for the students and their schools.

Marotta's book is a perfect companion to many of those listed here in that it translates leadership theories into tangible actions. For any practicing or aspiring school leaders, especially at the building level, it is highly recommended.

Bungay Stanier, Michael. 2016. *The Coaching Habit: Say Less, Ask More, and Change the Way You Lead Forever.* **Toronto: Box of Crayons Press.**

Michael Bungay Stanier's *The Coaching Habit* is centered on seven questions to help leaders transform their conversations and have a broader impact. Counterintuitively, this involves asking more open-ended questions to those we lead and providing less direct advice when helping people solve problems. School leaders often face overwhelm when they assume they are responsible for solving all problems within their purview. Rather than play the hero, *The Coaching Habit* recommends that leaders become better at helping others solve their own problems for themselves.

School leaders often pursue leadership positions because they want to help others. Great teachers want to help students and pursue school leadership because they want to broaden their impact on a larger school community. If unchecked, this drive to help can easily lead to burnout. Bungay Stanier recommends that leaders become more coach-like in their approach to leadership. Our habit is often to jump in and offer advice; the staff member receiving the advice may leave the office sooner, but they will more likely be back because they had their problem solved for them. Bungay Stanier recommends asking questions such as "What's on your mind?" and "What else could you do?" to help others think through solutions to their own challenges.

The final chapters are of value to school leaders as well. On page 205, the author discusses building a coaching habit over email. Instead of writing out long answers full of advice, Bungay Stanier advises leaders to apply the coaching conversation habits to this digital medium. His email starters are highly useful, such as "wow, there's a lot going on here. What's the real challenge for you, do you think?" (p. 205).

School leaders can easily promote an unhealthy email culture by attempting to reply quickly to all problems with lengthy advice. The message sent to stakeholders is, I am available at all times to solve all of your problems for you, just email them to me. Because it is more convenient for stakeholders to email than have a face-to-face conversation, email exchanges can rapidly proliferate. Applying these coaching techniques to email is one of Bungay Stanier's best takeaways.

Reframing leadership from problem-solving to coaching is useful for all school leaders. As school leaders ascend to building principal and district office positions, issues become more numerous and more complex. Assisting others to help them brainstorm their own solutions will help leaders build capacity and trust with their teams.

CHAPTER SUMMARY

These books would be an excellent follow-up to any certification program as new school leaders enter the administrative world. In addition, practicing school leaders would benefit as they encounter the day-to-day realities of high stress and high conflict work environments.

Overall, these books reinforce themes that were uncovered throughout the interview process and with the survey data.

- Building trusting relationships is the most important task any school leader can undertake. Nothing can move forward without trusting relationships.
- Identifying high-leverage activities and focusing time on those activities can make school leaders more effective.
- Listening and validating others' perspectives is a key leadership attribute.

Appendix
Survey Instrument

Question 1: What is your current leadership role?

- Principal
- Assistant Principal
- District Office—Director Level
- District Office—Assistant Superintendent Level
- Essential Service Provider
- Other

Question 2: How many years have you been in your current position?

Question 3: What best describes your current role level?

- Elementary School
- Middle Level
- High School
- Central/District Office

Question 4: Are you tenured in your current position?

- Yes
- No

Question 5: How many total years have you been in school leadership positions?

Question 6: How many total years have you been in education as a career?

Question 7: Gender Identification

- Female
- Male
- Choose Not to Say

Question 8: Marital Status

- Married
- Single
- Other

Question 9: Age Range

- 25–34
- 35–44
- 45–54
- 55–64
- 65+

Question 10: Number of children/dependents at home under thirteen years of age.

Question 11: Number of children/dependents at home between ages fourteen and twenty-five.

Question 12: What were your reasons for pursuing school leadership as a career choice? Please choose all that apply.

- Broader Impact on School Community
- Increased Pay
- Professional Challenge
- Increased Ability to Exert Influence
- Prestige
- Other

Question 13: If you chose "Other" for Question 12, please explain briefly below.

Question 14: How would you rate your overall level of satisfaction with your current leadership role?

- High
- Medium
- Low

Question 15: List the five most stressful tasks/dynamics/relationships you experience in your current leadership role?

Question 16: Of those five, which do you perceive is *least* within your ability to directly control?

Question 17: List the three most impact impactful "on-the-job" practices you have found to help fight back against work-related stress, burnout, and/or overload. These would be practices directly related to your leadership tasks.

Question 18: Of your answers to Question 17, which do you perceive as the "highest-leverage" activity—meaning, if you did this consistently and did it well, you would impact all other areas?

Question 19: List the three most impact impactful "outside-of-work" practices you have found to help fight back against work-related stress, burnout, and/or overload. These would be practices you pursue outside of regular work hours that impact your work-related stress.

Question 20: Of your answers to Question 19, which do you perceive as the "highest-leverage" activity—meaning, if you did this consistently and did it well, you would impact all other areas?

Question 21: Finally, if one of your employees said to you, "I want to go into school leadership," how strongly would you encourage them to pursue such a transition?

- Strongly Encourage
- Encourage
- Support in a Neutral Manner
- Discourage
- Strongly Discourage

About the Author

Dr. Larry Dake is a district-level administrator and an educational leadership professor in upstate New York. He has served as a secondary classroom teacher, curriculum coordinator, elementary building principal, and assistant superintendent over his sixteen-year educational career, with the last ten spent in leadership.

Dr. Dake became an administrator at age thirty and has struggled to navigate many of the areas outlined in this book. These experiences, plus his work preparing new leaders for administrative positions, were the inspiration for this book. Very quickly, it became apparent that formal certification programs are important, but other learning experiences were also necessary for success as a school leader.

Dr. Dake lives in upstate New York with his wife, Kelly, who is an elementary literacy teacher, and his three children, ages 11, 9, and 6.

www.ingramcontent.com/pod-product-compliance
Lightning Source LLC
Chambersburg PA
CBHW032030230426
43671CB00005B/264